Imagine
THAT!

Unlocking the Power of Your Imagination

Imagine
THAT!

Unlocking the Power of Your Imagination

by

DEWEY FRIEDEL

DESTINY IMAGE® PUBLISHERS, INC.
P.O. Box 310, Shippensburg, PA 17257-0310

*"Speaking to the Purposes of God for this Generation
and for the Generations to Come."*

This book and all other Destiny Image, Revival Press, Mercy Place, Fresh Bread, Destiny Image Fiction, and Treasure House books are available at Christian bookstores and distributors worldwide.

For a U.S. bookstore nearest you, call 1-800-722-6774.
For more information on foreign distributors, call 717-532-3040.
Or reach us on the Internet: www.destinyimage.com

ISBN 10: 0-7684-2413-5
ISBN 13: 978-0-7684-2413-3

For Worldwide Distribution, Printed in the U.S.A.

2 3 4 5 6 7 8 9 10 11 / 09 08 07

Endorsements

Once again Pastor Dewey Friedel places his thumb on the pulse of our subconscious. Kicking down the psychic walls that often confine us, *Imagine That!* empowers us to not only stretch the boundaries of our imagination, but grasp the multitude of prophetic threads within God's Word. We can see more if we would only believe more. But to believe more requires that we want more. This book has changed my life. I am certain it will change yours.

Bishop Donald Hilliard, Jr.
Senior Pastor, Cathedral International

Pastor Dewey Friedel's new book, *Imagine That!* is a must read for all Christians. God wants His children blessed, healthy, and prosperous in all areas of life. I truly believe this man of God has uncovered in the Scriptures one of the keys to our success as believers.

If we on earth want our children happy and fulfilled, how much more does our heavenly Father want us experiencing the same? Without the power of imagination and creativity, this planet and our current existence, would be very boring! Thank God for those who propagate faith as in

Hebrews 11:1 (NLV), *"Now faith is being sure we will get what we hope for. It is being sure of what we cannot see."*

The Trinity Broadcasting Network would not exist if it weren't for the God-given seeds of both "Faith" and "Imagination." Because my folks were simply obedient, Christian television is beaming around the world 24 hours a day, 7 days a week in dozens of different languages and dialects. After reading this book, I truly feel you will be better equipped to, "run the race" and "fight the good fight." We all need to know how to put our God-given talents to work and to understand that, *"the God who gives life to the dead, and calls things that are, not as though they were"* (Rom. 4:17).

Paul Crouch, Jr.
Vice President of Administration
Trinity Broadcasting Network

You are far more powerful than you ever imagined! Through this brilliantly worded, revelatory new work, Pastor Dewey Friedel has beautifully conveyed God's own heart about the power of our minds. Bravo Pastor Dewey!

Paula White
Co-pastor, Without Walls International Church
of Tampa, Florida

Outstanding! Very inspiring! Pastor Dewey captures the true essence of imagining your dreams to become a reality. With Christ in charge through faith, trust, and prayer, all dreams—if you believe—can come true. Just look around you and imagine God's creations and what it is going to be like in Heaven with eternal life.

Gary Carter
Baseball Hall of Fame Inductee 2003

Imagine That! may be one of the most important books you ever read. This exciting work proves, beyond the shadow of a doubt, that the human imagination is one of the most powerful natural and spiritual forces that exist. Full of exciting examples, natural evidence, and proven principles, this book will help you believe, achieve, and receive exceedingly and abundantly more than you previously imagined—take this dynamic journey and rejoice for the great things that await you.

Pastor Tommy Barnett
Phoenix First Assembly & L.A. Dream Center

As a psychiatrist, I ask all new patients, "What is your goal in life?" The younger generation usually say, "I don't have one," or "Just to enjoy today." I also ask them what they tell themselves when they make a mistake, and what they tell their best friend when she makes a similar mistake. The answers are usually harsh on self, but kind to the friend, so the patient is lying to either friend or self. By deciding that moment to treat *self* as a friend from that point forward, and to think of reasonable but exciting goals in life, the patient can have a dramatically improved quality of life in just a few minutes of redecisions. I am very excited that my friend,

Dewey Friedel, has written *Imagine That!* It will be life changing to all who read it and heed it.

Paul Meier, M.D.
Author of 72 books and founder of Meier Clinics

Dewey Friedel is one of the most qualified people, I believe, in the Christian world and is able to bring this truth to believers and non-believers at the same time. As the subject of the imagination seems to be a major topic of readers throughout the world today it is very necessary for it to be dealt with on a biblical, easy-to-read revelation basis. We must all live in our imagination of the future, rather than in our past. I highly recommend this book as a fresh insight and dynamic way to deal with prayer, faith, dreams, and abundant life.

Ray McCauley
Senior Pastor and Founder
Rhema Ministries South Africa

Table of Contents

Preface

In 1981 I experienced a major breakthrough both in knowledge and in experience. This happened when my wife, Ronda, and I were teaching pastors in Kenya, Africa, under the great leadership of Kenya's Bishop Silas Owiti. We were also engaged in evangelistic ministry there. As we ministered, we were eyewitnesses of numerous miracles, which were very much like the ones we read about in the Gospels and the Book of Acts.

As I saw God's hand at work, I couldn't help but wish that all my professors who taught me at Princeton Theological Seminary could have been in the primitive bush country with me so they could see what we were seeing and experiencing—a reality that they had relegated to the realm of mythology and symbolism.

Many of my professors had been influenced by "higher criticism," especially the theology of Rudolf Bultmann. Their world view and paradigm would have experienced a shock or "mind quake" that would have been devastating in a healthy way had they been able to see what my wife and I had seen in Kenya. As we concluded our ministry there, Ronda and I traveled to Seoul, Korea, where the founder of Logos International and the *Logos Journal*, Dan Malachuk, had arranged for us to have a personal appointment with Dr. Paul Yonggi Cho (now Dr. David Yonggi Cho), and learn from his teaching as we attended one of this great pastor's seminars.

Dr. Cho had challenged us through the use of Old Testament Scriptures regarding Abraham and Jacob to use visualization to help us grow in faith and to experience church growth, as well. Most of the material Dr. Cho presented had been covered in his best-selling book, *The Fourth Dimension.*

The principles he shared in the seminar certainly are practical, as is evidenced by the fact that Dr. Cho's church— Yoido Full Gospel Church— is the largest Christian church in the world, and he attributes all the growth of the church he pastors to these primarily Old Testament principles.

It was wonderful to be exposed to his anointed ministry. When we left Seoul, Korea, we returned to New Jersey to build a great church with a great school. Sadly, though, within a short time, Dr. Cho's teachings became just a distant memory to us, with only bits and pieces being incorporated into our daily ministry. We were so involved in building the church that we forgot the basic church-building principles we had learned.

It wasn't until recently that I realized that when our school, family life center, and beautiful baseball facility were completed in 1999, the principles Dr. Cho had taught us had been subconsciously influencing us all along, as we built the buildings that are central to our ministry. It also dawned on me that we had imagined "things hoped for" in prayer and that these hoped-for things had become material realities. At the same time, however, it became clear to me that we had not used these same principles for actual church growth, but only for the building of the facilities.

Therefore, it is somewhat surprising to me that our church, which is not a mega-church, has had such a great influence in the state of New Jersey, especially among local and state government officials, celebrities, and educators. Certainly we are a large church for our particular geographical area, but our size does not compare with the mega-churches with memberships in the thousands in various urban areas across the U.S.A.

When I consider all the miracles it took to overcome the heavy opposition we faced in our modern, intellectual, non-Bible-belt region, I began to wonder what would really happen if people gained more insights from the New Testament with regard to goals, desires, and the imagination—principles that are necessary to manifest God's dreams for our lives.

It occurred to me that if Dr. Cho's church grew to be so large based on Old Testament principles, what limitless possibilities might there be if we went beyond Abraham, Jacob, and Joseph, from whose lives and stories he gained great techniques and inspiration. Therefore, I started a scriptural study on this important matter, and I discovered that the imagination was employed in many pivotal places throughout the Bible. I learned that many times the King James translators would translate the Hebrew or Greek words for "imagination" as "mind" or "heart."

It all started to make sense to me then, both in my rational mind and within my spirit. Let's look at just a few examples before we start to examine them more fully in the following chapters. Since I've begun implementing some of these principles on imagination, I have met significant people who are helping me to double my real-estate investments along with others who are offering us millions of dollars for property that they really need to complete their own project!

Our people at Shore Christian Center have entered a realm of new joy in prayer, and they are experiencing a new hunger for God. In fact, our area has become very spiritually hungry indeed. People are coming to the Lord more freely and easily than they ever did before. For example, one of our guests a few months ago had been the concert organ player for the legendary guitarist Jimmy Hendrix. This talented organist became a Christian during an offering I was taking during one of our summer services.

When someone gets saved during an offering, you know that something good is up! In just a few months since incorporating these principle in my own life and ministry, I've experienced unusual TV offers, publishing opportunities, invitations to speak at some of the largest churches in the world, and our church helped break a curse over one athlete who went on to sign a 50-million-dollar contract this past summer!

Now are you interested? Of course you are! Keep on reading. The law of faith and imagination is for all of God's children, including you!

As I'm sitting on the balcony of our condo and looking at the sunbeams bouncing off the beautiful waters of the San Carlos Bay, I have been thinking about you, my reader. What you are about to discover will be a turning point in your life. When my Christian friends "get over the fear of the water" and in a fresh way become disciples (disciplined learners), they will internally jump with the excitement of a dynamic, new way to think about prayer, faith, having their dreams manifested, and the sheer ecstasy of abundant life here in this existence, not just in the one to come.

And, when my new-age, higher-consciousness or even agnostic seeker friends learn what Jesus and the Bible have to say about imagination, perhaps they will gladly welcome not an impersonal, benevolent universe, but rejoice in an objective God-man (Jesus) who loves them and has left clues to His personhood and His desire to connect with them all through their short or long journeys of life.

Sometimes my agnostic and Christian friends are much more alike than they care to admit. So often both are locked within a statistical world, the so-called world of reality. Both are fond of seeing themselves as being realistic people. Then they get locked into a statistical "world box," bowing before "facts."

Only the evangelicals and charismatics get to enjoy an occasional miracle here and there, but most of their emphasis is on "slugging it out" with the world of facts until the Rapture or Heaven envelops them in bliss. They long for a life in which they can finally gain control and not have to be a pawn for supposed bad corporations or the destructive evil of a world gone mad with the toxic-sin cocktails people are drinking every day due to the devil's influence.

I like what Wolfgang Pauli, the Nobel Prize-winning physicist, said about reality, "The layman usually means something obvious and well-known, whereas it seems to me that precisely the most important and extremely difficult task of our time is to work on elaborating a new idea of reality. This is also what I mean when I always emphasize that science and religion must be related in some way."

I want you, my reader, to really enjoy this book. Without a doubt, you will develop hope and grow in faith as you've never done before. There will be ample support both scientifically and scripturally for you to put these turning points into practice in your own life. Of course there is the awesome, powerful potential of these few pages of insight becoming a "paradigm-buster" in your life. (A paradigm is an internally consistent framework in which we function.) The truths I'm about to share with you have the potential to lead you "out of the box," enabling you to experience a truly revolutionary lifestyle.

Now, to my friends in the "Faith Movement," you will see what has been a missing part in the development of personal faith. Jesus has led you to a great treasure that is found in Hebrews 11 and Mark 11, but start digging at the site, if you really want to experience the rewards of faith.

Finally, to anyone who is reading this book with a desire to stir up hope in your life again—this is a great opportunity for you to do so. You may be hopping from church to church, or maybe you left the synagogue, or perhaps you're just disappointed with endless awareness principles that are not manifesting in your life. If you accept what is presented in this book, it will permanently change the way you see things, I promise.

Never again will you be the victim of forces beyond your control. You will team up with the universe and the God of the universe and co-create reality. Can you imagine that? Ultimately, as you will see, this will be easy, for *"as he* [any person] *thinketh in his heart, so is he"* (Prov. 23:7 KJV).

Introduction

During the last 20 years or so, my wife and I have seen the manifestation of many of our personal dreams. So many things have materialized from extreme personal blessings to the enjoyment of seeing the fruit of hundreds of changed lives that have come from overseeing an influential church with its "Broadway at the Shore" plays, to the sports clinics with the pros at our state-of-the-art facilities, and a school that continues to get state-wide recognition.

In addition, I was able to write a six-figure check this past December to our favorite charity, and we've been able to help thousands of people through TV tapes and the purchase of vehicles for international ministries. All of these blessings have come about as a result of creative prayer.

"LET'S HEAR THE BASKETBALLS BOUNCING!"

I remember clearly saying to our students one day in Shore Christian Academy—"Now, let's just hear the basketballs bouncing on the gymnasium floor!" That was all well and good, but the problem was that we didn't have a gymnasium! However, we imagined it as we prayed until it came to pass.

While we used creative prayer, I mysteriously met a man in a crowd of 3,000 people who became the catalyst that enabled the field house to materialize. You may ask, "Oh, what is this, just more of that mind over matter stuff?" Yes, it's that and so much more!

In 1987 physicist Robert G. Jahn and clinical psychologist Brenda J. Dunne, who both worked at Princeton University, announced that they had accumulated unequivocal evidence that the mind can psychically interact with physical reality. More specifically, they found that through mental concentration alone people are able to affect the way certain kinds of machines operate.[1]

THE LAW OF INCREASE

Certainly this is really important news and cannot be accounted for in terms of our standard picture of reality. Scientists are beginning to confirm the existence of certain spiritual laws such as the law of increase, which states that whatever you are truly grateful for and appreciate will increase in your life. But, there is also a dark flip side to this principle: the negative emotions you broadcast—anger, distrust, hate, jealousy, etc. are also picked up and reflected back to you with greater force.

In other words, the universe is like a vast Dolby surround-sound system. It picks up what you emit, greatly increases its power, and beams it back to you. We know this intuitively and that is the reason we commonly say things like, "You reap what you sow," "It's payback time," and "What goes around comes around." So many of us have used this power unconsciously, often in negative and unwise ways.

Introduction

THE "OTHER REALITY"

After years of firsthand experience, biologist Lyall Watson said, "I have no doubt that reality is in a very large part, a construct of the imagination. I think we have the capacity to change the world around us in quite fundamental ways."[2] This "other reality," I call it, is now being a little better understood. All of us have heard about "vibes." Even the Beach Boys had a hit song entitled, "Good Vibrations."

All of us have felt vibes coming from other people at a party, a dinner engagement, or a job interview. Over the past 20 years, Valerie Hunt, a physical therapist and professor of kinesiology at UCLA, has developed a way to confirm experimentally the existence of the human energy field. Medical science has long known that humans are electromagnetic beings. Doctors routinely use electrocardiographs to make electrocardiograms (EKGs) or records of the electrical activity of the heart and electroencephalographs (EEGs) to record the brain's electrical activity.

Dr. Hunt has discovered that an electromyograph, a device used to measure the electrical activity in the muscles, can also pick up the electrical presence of the human energy field.[3] Could it be possible that wonderful vibes that are released from a person could attract miracles of answered prayer? Could there be a form of creative prayer that has been somewhat hidden to most of us? It is commonly believed that cats purr when content. However, cats also purr when they are severely injured, frightened, or giving birth. Now scientists are discovering that the purr of the cat is a healing vibrational stimulation. After a day or night of hunting, purring could be likened to an internal vibrational therapeutic system, a sort of kitty massage that keeps muscles and ligaments in prime condition and less prone to injury. It is even thought that the purr can strengthen the bone and prevent diseases. Following injury, the purr vibrations help heal the wound or bone associated with the injury, reduce the swelling, and provide some pain relief during the healing process. What is to stop you from developing vibrations that could help you achieve nine lives like your pets? Why not? Keep reading. It gets even better!

THE "STRING THEORY"

In our post-Einstein world, a sizable part of the physics and mathematics community has become increasingly convinced that the "String Theory" is the unified theory of everything that Einstein was searching for. The String Theory holds that everything at its most microscopic level consists of combinations of vibrating strands. The strings on a violin or a piano have resonant frequencies at which they prefer to vibrate—patterns that our ears sense as various musical notes and their higher harmonics; the same holds true for atoms, which in turn are made from quarks and electrons—*electrons* (remember, everything involves electricity)—and all such particles are actually loops of vibrating strings.

It seems as if there is a song that is constantly playing in God's vast creation. The heavens do declare His handiwork in perfect harmony like a great cosmic symphony. This is the ancient Pythagorean "music of the spheres." The String Theory suggests that the microscopic landscape is filled with tiny strings whose vibrational patterns orchestrate the order of the cosmos.

THE POWER OF THOUGHT

The world gasped at the devastating and destructive power arising from the conversion of less than 1 percent of two pounds of uranium into energy at Hiroshima in 1945. Could it be that we may be on the verge of using the secret power of the atom to create a world where the glory of the Lord covers the earth as the waters cover the sea?

The power of thought is the only thing over which you have control. A definite strong idea, when held consistently in the imagination, can actually change the biochemistry of the brain so that it will no longer be programmed for failure or defeat. Thoughts are things, and our thoughts become words. In the Hebrew language *dabar* means both "word" and "thing." Thoughts have an electromagnetic reality, and they create their visible counterpart in the outer world. If you can change what you think—what you imagine—your conditions will also change. Sigmund Freud said, "In our unconscious mind we cannot distinguish between a wish and a deed."[4]

Let's say you are riding down the street and you pass by a Starbucks coffee shop. Your thoughts start to imagine the delicious taste of a vanilla frappachino mixed with one of the tasty pastries of the day. At that moment you pick up a vibration that will be in harmony with certain brain cells related to those stimuli, and the neurons within your brain will begin firing. When their amplitude becomes heightened above a certain level, a "rocket of desire" will be launched within you, and then you will have to decide what is more important—your waistline or filling your mouth with fleeting happiness.

Sometimes the desire is so great and your imagination is so strong that your car seems uncontrollable and it seems to turn into Starbucks almost by itself! Ha! As you are munching down the epicurean tidbit and slowly swallowing the hybrid coffee, it is as if your thought was a thing—at least it became one—a tangible manifestation of your desire.

Scientists are seeing that thoughts and mental images can initiate physiological changes in our bodies. Dr. Thurman Fleet says, "Man must take responsibility for the state of his body for we are the product of our thought creations."[5] We know that by changing the vibrations of something, you can change its condition. If even disease and health involve vibrations, disease can be conquered by changing a vibration or applying energy on the material plane. Ice can be changed into water by applying energy in the form of heat. Now the same water can become steam when we step up its vibrations.

Dr. Irving Oyle states: "By changing the consciousness, the mental picture you have of what is going on in your body, you can change the physical body. There is a certain type of personality that tends to get heart attacks. If you can think yourself into them, why can't you think yourself out of them?"[6]

In the field of sports we also find this important key at work! Former top seed/professional tennis player, Chris Evert, said that before every match she sat down and imagined her every move and she imagined returning every one of her opponent's volleys, eventually winning the match in her imagination, which resulted in her often winning the match in reality.

From Michael Jordan to Tiger Woods, great stars have testified to the successful use of their imaginations. Recently my good friend Gary Carter told me that, as a young teenager, he used to dream of receiving the honor of being inducted into the Hall of Fame in Cooperstown, and one day he did. My wife and I were his guests, and we watched with pride as this wonderful man was inducted into Cooperstown's Hall of Fame, where baseball's elite are honored.

Dr. Charles Garfield, a psychologist at the University of California in Berkeley, said, "The key is to visualize yourself with the clarity necessary to really feel yourself in the situation. The central nervous system doesn't know the difference between deep, powerful visualization and the event itself, so the physical follow-up of the actual event is merely an after-the-fact duplication of an event already performed and completed in imagery."[7]

In one study of world-class Soviet athletes, the stars were divided into four groups. The first group spent 100 percent of their training time in actual training. The second group spent 75 percent of their time training and 25 percent of their time imagining the exact movements and accomplishments they wanted to achieve in the sport. The third group spent 50 percent of their time training and 50 percent using their imaginations, and the fourth group spent 25 percent training and 75 percent imagining. During the 1980 Winter Games in Lake Placid, New York, the fourth group showed the greatest improvement in performance, followed by groups three, two, and one in that order! Perhaps there is more truth than we ever imagined in the Apollo 14 astronaut Captain Edgar Mitchell's words: "The single secret of the universe is you create your own reality."[8]

I have included in this introduction a little scientific evidence of the power of your imagination, but for the most part I will be using my own background and experience in Biblical studies to establish a case for the use of your imagination. When you see the Scriptures, it will become as obvious to you as the air you breathe is. You will not be bored with physics or biology lessons, but you will reach a certain height where there are no clouds. You will learn how every day you can soar above the clouds through your imagination, and that what you thought was fiction or fantasy can become concrete fact. You will see that faith includes imagination and it must do so in order for the things you hope for to become manifested evidence.

Some of you are still afraid of the water and will be quick to label this as heretical before ever looking at the evidence that is easily found in the Judeo-Christian Scriptures. Take some time to become a disciplined learner, and you will understand that whether it is Billy Graham seeing and imagining the harvest of millions of souls or Oral Roberts walking the farmland adjacent to South Lewis Avenue in Tulsa, Oklahoma, many years ago, as he envisioned and imagined a great university when there was no money in his pocket and no deed in his hand, that these men prayed and imagined something so vividly and passionately that the facts of their vision eventually materialized. Similarly, you will understand why Walt Disney's focused imagination brought fantasyland to earth.

No matter what field of endeavor you hope to enter, when you do so with the law of faith and the free use of your imagination, you will more than succeed. You will have super, world-changing, and eye-opening success.

Now, happy reading. Get to it and I will see you at the top of your dreams. As you do so, remember what the late A.W. Tozer said, "Paul was a seeker, a finder, and a seeker still."[9] Keep seeking and you will find. You have been knocking long enough, and now the door is about to open in your life. Imagine that!

ENDNOTES

1. Robert G. Jahn, Brenda J. Dunne, and Michael Talbot, *The Holographic Universe* (New York: 1992), 5.

2. Lyall Watson and Michael Talbot, *The Holographic Universe* (New York, 1992), Ibid., 138.

3. Valerie Hunt and Michael Talbot, *The Holographic Universe* (New York: 1992), Ibid.,174.

4. Sigmund Freud and Marta Hiatt, *Mind Magic* (St. Paul, MN: 2005), 31.

5. Thurman Fleet, and Marta Hiatt, *Mind Magic* (St. Paul, MN: 2005), Ibid., 156.

6. Irving Oyle and Marta Hiatt, *Mind Magic* (St. Paul, MN: 2005), Ibid., 152, 153.

7. Charles Garfield and Marta Hiatt, *Mind Magic* (St. Paul, MN: 2005), Ibid., 74.

8. Edgar Mitchell and Marta Hiatt, *Mind Magic* (St. Paul, MN: 2005), Ibid., intro. XVI.

9. A.W. Tozer, *Gems From Tozer* (London, England: 1969), 19.

CHAPTER 1

The Key to Your Imagination

Most of the world's greatest achievers constantly pictured in their minds what they wanted. Their subconscious minds had something to work on, and, as a result, their desires were eventually manifested. All of us are directly or indirectly responsible for almost everything that happens to us. The way we think and feel has an intimate connection with our daily circumstances.

Many of you have been taught so many negative concepts about yourself that you automatically expect and imagine the worst, so you create difficulties and limitations for yourself and others. Many Christians think that confession of the Word is everything, while missing out on all the Bible has to say about what is necessary before we actually decree a word.

One woman who was overweight, for example, had placed a picture of a huge hippopotamus on her refrigerator door. By doing so she was simply telling her subconscious mind that she was a fat hippo! You have to let your subconscious know what you want, not what you don't want. If the woman wanted to continue looking like Petunia Pig, then the picture of the hippo was fine; if not, she should have pasted a more appropriate model before her eyes each day. Albert

Schweitzer said, "The greatest discovery of this generation is that human beings can alter their lives by altering their attitude of mind."[1]

LOVE GOD WITH ALL OF YOUR IMAGINATION

God has given you a mind with untapped potential that goes far beyond your everyday uses of it. Dr. Franz Inglefinger, former editor of the *New England Journal of Medicine*, stated that 85 percent of all people who bring complaints and symptoms to their physicians suffer from self-limiting disorders.[2] So a disease is not just merely a physical problem that is isolated in your body, but a problem of your whole person—spirit, mind, and body. The Bible has a lot to say about this truth, but we have misused much of this information because often where the King James translators give us the words "heart" and "mind," the actual translation of the Greek or Hebrew word is much closer to our English word "imagination."

Matthew 22:37 states, *"Jesus said to him, 'You shall love the Lord your God with all your heart, with all your soul, and with all your mind.'"* The Greek word for "mind" in this verse is dionoia, and it clearly means "imagination." God wants you to love Him completely with all your imagination.

Paul said something similar in Philippians 4:8: *"Finally, brethren, whatever things are true, whatever things are noble, whatever things are just, whatever things are pure, whatever things are lovely, whatever things are of a good report, if there is any virtue and if there is anything praiseworthy—**meditate** on these things."*

The Greek word for meditation is *meletao*, and it also means "to imagine." My wife and I knew a woman who was beginning to despise her husband. This verse turned her marriage around. It says if there is anything praiseworthy, meditate on that. She could only find one thing about her husband that she actually liked; one thing that she considered to be praiseworthy. She began to imagine this one attribute every time she thought of him. As a result, her negative thoughts about him were canceled out by the use of her imagination, and their marriage was wonderfully restored.

GIRD UP THE LOINS OF YOUR MIND

In First Peter 1:13 we read, "*Therefore gird up the loins of your mind...*". Usually no one thinks of loins as being in your mind. Your loins are located in the abdominal region of your body and they house your reproductive organs. Notice that the Greek word for "mind" in this verse is *dionoia*— imagination. Yes, your imagination (the loins of your mind) is a reproductive area which brings you the abundant life that Jesus promised. Did you see that? Look again!

The Bible says, "*These all died in faith, not having received the promises, but having seen them afar off were assured of them, embraced them and confessed that they were strangers and pilgrims on the earth*" (Heb. 11:13). Verse 40 of that same chapter says, "*God having provided something better for us....*"

Since the Resurrection of Jesus Christ, a new day has come for believers. We can now receive the promises as we see them, being fully assured of them, embracing them, and then confessing them. Today nothing can separate us from the love of Christ, and His promise for us is part of His love toward us. Whether it be tribulation, distress, persecution, or any other kind of trouble in "*all these things we are more than conquerors through Him who loved us*" (Rom. 8:37).

Renew Your Mind

In order to experience this level of victorious living we must bring it to pass through the reproductive part of our minds—our imaginations. This is what enables you "to see afar off." First, you picture the promise being fulfilled in your mind. Paul also tells us to renew our minds. (See Romans 12:2.) The Greek word that is translated as "renew" in this verse means "with intensity and with repetition."

If you program your subconscious mind consistently with great emotion and dedication, you will see God's promises fulfilled in your life, and you will reach the awesome height of your destiny. Many people talk about their purpose-driven life, but they don't know how to drive their purpose from one level to the next. The vehicle for doing so is the loins of your mind. Your imagination will produce whatever pictures you consistently put before it.

Joshua 1:8 says, *"This Book of the Law shall not depart from your mouth, but you shall meditate in it day and night, that you may observe to do according to all that is written in it. For then you will make your way prosperous, and then you will have good success."* The word translated as "meditate" in this verse is *hagah,* and it means "to ponder or to imagine." Go ahead now; look up all these verses in a concordance for yourself. You will see!

There is much more to come; as a matter of fact, I am so eager to get this knowledge to you that I might even become a little "teachy-preachy" in the next chapters. You have been living on a lower plane than God intended for you. Now you are going to rise up with great excitement and really become the head and not the tail. (See Deuteronomy 28:13.)

Many of you have been frustrated and disappointed. You have confessed one thing and received another. Mark 11:24 says, *"Therefore I tell you, whatever you ask for in prayer, believe that you have received it, and it will be yours"* (NIV). Notice the tense of the verb "receive." It is in the past tense. You must produce the pictures of receiving what you ask for with joy in your mind—within your *dionoia*—your imagination. This is the real place of your heart.

When your imagination rules your heart, you will receive what you have daydreamed, night dreamed, and consistently burnt into your mind. Don't count yourself out; this is for the rocket scientist as well as for the garbage collector. Henry Ford didn't finish high school, and neither did Thomas Edison. Bill Gates dropped out of college to pursue his dream. Paula White was told she would be in a mental institution for the rest of her life. And I was told by my first-grade teacher that I wasn't smart enough to finish school! Well, this bed-wetting little dumb boy was inducted into the National Honor Society, received several scholarships, and made it through Princeton Theological Seminary without any grades lower than a "B." Now imagine that!

ENDNOTES

1. Albert Schweitzer, Hiatt, OP-CIT. intro p. XIII.

2. Franz Inglefinger, *New England Journal of Medicine* Hiatt, OP-CIT. intro. Ibid., 146.

CHAPTER 2

Three Active Ingredients

I am indebted to Dr. David Yonggi Cho for the three ingredients I cover in this chapter.

In the first chapter of Genesis, God has given us a tremendous principle and a great secret, so let's take a look at the first three verses of the Bible: *"In the beginning God created the heavens and the earth. The earth was without form, and void; and darkness was on the face of the deep. And the Spirit of God was hovering over the face of the waters."*

Now take a look at your own life, and you may discover that you are in some tough places that seem very dark indeed. For example, you may have prayed some prayers that haven't yet been answered. There's a sense in which you may consider yourself to be in "the place of the void." That's a place where you may say, "God, I just don't understand this. I haven't received anything from you in this area. And I've been working on it for a long time. I've been giving in that area, but I don't see anything! God, it's like darkness to me. I'm in the void—in the deep, the very face of the deep!"

A TIME OF BROODING

Did you know that the Holy Spirit broods over the deep and dark void in your life? The Holy Spirit hovered over the water in Genesis 1, and this means that He was brooding or "incubating" over the waters. It's an image that's very similar to a mother hen sitting on an egg. She keeps waiting, brooding, hovering, and incubating until the egg is hatched.

That's what brooding is all about. Perhaps you are just about to enter a place of brooding in your life, because you're waiting for the hatching of a dream that God ordained for your life before the world was formed. You have to go through the hatching process first, however. This might tempt some to say, "Why does it have to be so tough?" Remember that it's in the darkness, in the crisis, in the void, where the Holy Spirit broods and incubates. It is there where He begins to work in your behalf.

Look at what happened during the Creation. "*God said, 'Let there be light,' and there was light*" (Gen. 1:3). You must learn to wait for a word from God—the word within the Word that will suddenly become light to you.

You may then be able to say, "I don't know why, but now I believe, and it's so easy to believe God in this area." This confirms what the Bible says: "*Now faith is the substance of things hoped for…*" (Heb. 11:1). What is the meaning of the word "substance," as it is used here? I believe you could break it down into the following three ingredients.

A Clear-Cut Goal

*N*umber one: You need a very clear-cut goal so your faith can rise to the occasion. And, as soon as you get a clear-cut goal related to the dream God wants you to fulfill in your life, a tsunami-like attack will come against it. The enemy will come against the fulfillment of your dream with full force. It is then when you will experience the winds of adversity. The devil will try to stop you through fear and doubt and any other means he will come up with.

Without a powerful, strong goal for your faith to focus on, you will have no substance with which to pray. Remember, faith is the substance of things hoped for. What are you hoping for? Write it down. Get a piece of paper and write down your faith-goal. Make it clear, specific, and practical, not vague.

Is your goal in the realm of healing? What do you want? Jesus knew that blind Bartemeaus was sightless; nonetheless he asked him, "What do you want me to do for you?" The blind man answered, "...*that I may receive my sight*" (Mark 10:51). Remember, Jesus wants you to ask very specifically.

If you are a woman who is praying for a man, for example, be sure to ask specifically. Specify the height, weight, and career that you would like the "man of your dreams" to have. You may laugh at this suggestion, but being specific is very important when it comes to your dreams.

When you begin to ask specific things from God, He begins to create the answer for you. He starts to work toward the fulfillment of your dream, because He put it in your heart in the first place. It's not just a whim. God put it there. Therefore, it's important for you to discover what God has put in your heart. Make it into a clear-cut goal.

When your goal is clear, it will become like a lighthouse in a storm. You can see it during the storm even though darkness and fog surround you.

A lot of people are wishy-washy about their goals. They don't really know what their goals are. Jesus is saying, "What do you want me to do for you?"

You might respond, "Well, I'd like to be blessed." Well, what kind of blessing are you looking for?

THE ROLE OF DESIRE

The *number two* ingredient you must have in order to see your dreams and goals materialize is a tremendous desire to fulfill your goal. Most people experience only passing desires and then the next day they move on to something different. They wonder, "What was it that I said I wanted yesterday? I don't even remember what it was. Oh, well, it must not have been very important!"

They had a passing desire and they forgot their goal. They got their eyes off the prize, so to speak. Others may have just a lukewarm desire. In order to see the fulfillment of your dreams you must have a strong, powerful faith; this is the way you receive answers to your prayers.

You won't be able to maintain such a strong faith, however, unless you give it substance in the form of a strong desire. Turn that knob up on the stove. Turn it to high. Make it very high. In fact, get it as hot as you can. Say, "Holy Spirit, pour your heat on me in this area." That's His job, you know. The Holy Spirit's job is to ignite you, to set you on fire He wants to create a fire of passion in your heart for the very thing you desire.

VISIONS AND DREAMS

The *third* ingredient, likewise, is very important: *visions and dreams*. We don't have to get spooky about this by walking around and saying, "Oh, I'm having a vision." No, the kinds of dreams and visions I'm referring to are developed in your mind, in your heart, and in your spirit. They are birthed in the realm of your imagination.

Never forget that the Spirit of God has a language. Joel said, "*And it shall come to pass afterward that I will pour out My Spirit on all flesh; your sons and your daughters shall prophesy, your old men shall dream dreams, your young men shall see visions. And also on My menservants and on My maidservants I will pour out My Spirit in those days*" (Joel 2:28-29).

In the last days, which actually began on the Day of Pentecost, God said He would pour out His Spirit upon all flesh. When this happens, your young men will see visions and your old men will dream dreams. Your sons and daughters will prophesy the Word of the living God, the Word that He has for specific areas of your life.

God has a dream for your life that needs to be hatched. And He has a way of getting that dream fulfilled. Therefore, you should begin to visualize your goal, your dream coming true. That's why God gave you an imagination. Your imagination is incredibly powerful. Jesus said that if you look upon a woman with lust, it's the same as if you did the very act.

Let all preachers beware of that truth when they're condemning everybody on television. By so doing they're putting forth the power of the imagination in the negative. Instead, always be sure to take that power in positive directions; then you will see the manifestation you're looking for. The Holy Spirit will come and help you in that area as you step forth with a faith-filled imagination that has been set ablaze by the Holy Spirit.

Imagine THAT!

FELLOWSHIP AND COMMUNION WITH THE HOLY SPIRIT

What creates fellowship and communion with the Holy Spirit? To have fellowship and communion with Him we must know His language. What is the language of the Spirit? It is the language of dreams; the language of imagination that enables you to see something in the spirit realm before it is manifested in the physical realm.

When you begin to see it in the spirit, it becomes very real to you. So be sure to get a clear-cut goal. Pray that God will send fire on that goal in order to ignite it into a full-flamed passion in your life. You might even want to pray as follows: "Lord, let me feel it. Let it burn in my life!"

Then begin to let your dreams guide you. See your goal every day and several times a day. Before long you will experience the joy of seeing your dream fulfilled.

I heard the balls bouncing on the basketball court of our church's gymnasium before there ever was a gym in our Family Life Center. I heard it and I dreamed it. I persevered with this dream even though we were turned down time and time again by the township zoning board. Nonetheless, we'd still meet with our students and say, "Kids, we're going to see that school, we're going to see that basketball court, we're going to see that gymnasium." Why was I able to say these things to them? It was simply because I saw it as though it had already come to pass. I saw with the eyes of my spirit.

You have to picture those basketballs bouncing on the floor of your dream. Don't sit there passively. You've got to see it fulfilled. Remember the three ingredients I've outlined in this chapter—a *clear-cut goal,* a *strong desire,* and the experience of *dreams and visions.* When you get these in order in your life—your goal, your desire for that goal, and speaking the same language as God's Holy Spirit in visions and dreams, then one day, you're going to wake up and say, "I don't know why, I just know it's going to happen. I just know that I know. Because now I've got faith to see an answer to my prayer. Before I was just saying words, but now I've actually seen it come to pass. I've heard it in my spirit, so I believe it now. And when you believe it, it shall be done unto you according to your faith. Even when you're in the valley of darkness, hold on to your belief.

COMMANDING PRAYER

When these three ingredients line up, and you finally see the fulfillment of your dream in your imagination, and you have faith for it, your prayer will turn into what I call a "commanding prayer." This is the kind of prayer Jesus taught us to pray when He said, "...*If you have faith as a mustard seed, you will say to this mountain, 'Move from here to there,' and it will move; and nothing will be impossible for you"* (Matt. 17:20).

How can we really believe what we're praying for? You must make sure your goal is clear. Remind yourself of it constantly by putting it on your refrigerator. Put it on your notebook. Put it in your briefcase. Put it in your Bible. And then say, "God, I may not feel very heated about this right now, but I'm asking you to do what is necessary within me."

The Holy Spirit loves to answer that prayer, and He'll turn up the heat. The fire will start to burn. Then you will say, "Lord, thank you that I have the ability to imagine and to daydream about this thing even when it's dark on the outside."

What I'm describing here is so much more than a feeling sensation. It actually becomes a spiritual language in your life even in times of "outer darkness." Faith likes to work in darkness, because that's where the Holy Spirit incubates until the particular word of God that's in your imagination materializes. When that happens, an explosion will take place!

Faith is choosing to believe that God is going to turn the situation around. Abraham could not believe that at the age of 85 he could impregnate his old wife. He, too, was a "senior citizen"! But God had to get him out of the tent. God had to tap him on the shoulder and say, "Abraham, tonight you're getting up. I can't let you stay in your comfort zone. I can't speak to you in your comfort zone, because you've developed a whole pattern of unbelief. I told you that you're going to have a son—a natural son." (See Genesis 15.)

Abraham had a hard time believing what God was telling him because he was looking through the lens of his natural life. God had to get him out of the tent. When He did so, He was able to get Abraham to look up, and when the old man saw the stars in the sky, God told him that He would make his descendants as numerous as those heavenly bodies!

Abraham must have seen the children's faces in those stars. God had shown him something visually, and that picture must have become strong in his imagination. And the Bible says that when the old patriarch beheld that vision, he was finally able to say, "I believe you, God." It was then that his faith was reckoned unto him as righteousness.

It will be the same with you when you start to see what God has in store for you. Imagine it. And one day you're going to have the faith to believe it will come to pass, because you will have a picture painted on the canvas of your heart. Then you will pray with faith. Always remember that without faith your prayers are nothing. But with faith and persistence you will enter the destiny that God has made for you. You'll break down all the walls of impossibility and you'll enter a whole new dimension of life.

LET YOUR IMAGINATION GIVE BIRTH TO GOD'S REVELATION

Sometimes when we pray, we simply don't believe. We don't believe that God can bless our family, our mother, our father, our brother, our sister, our uncle, our aunt, our granddaddy, our cousins, our spouses, our friends, our neighbors, and our co-workers. We think, "But will He?" There is absolutely no faith in that question. On the other hand, if you imagine the ones you're praying for raising their hands and praising the Lord, see them walking down an aisle to receive Jesus, sitting in front of a television set and suddenly hearing the Holy Spirit come out of the words of a man or woman of God, and you see them say yes, then you've taken the first steps toward having your prayers answered. Say, "Lord, I see it." Let your imagination give birth to His revelation. It's unfolding and being unveiled for the ones you're holding in your prayers.

In the same way that Abraham had to come out of the tent in order to see the vision, some people have to come out of where they are in order to see what God has for them. They need to have a clear-cut goal. Only then will they see it accomplished in their lives.

When you're under attack for your dream, you can say, "This is my goal, satan! God gave it to me. I choose to keep looking at the prize, not at the problem. I'm not in the dark hole of doubt and fear any more; I'm living in the realm of the goal. Not the dark hole, but the goal!"

Then you will be able to say, "Lord, I thank you. Holy Spirit, I want to commune with you. Heat up this desire so that when I pray it, something will light up on the inside of me.

As I write these words, I'm praying that some of my readers will start making $50,000 a month. Can you believe God for that? Somebody might say, "Oh, that's so materialistic!" My response to them is, "No, it's not materialistic—not when you have the Kingdom of God in mind. There are things that have to be done. Hundreds of thousands of people need to be helped. People who make $50,000 a month will be able to help them. God wants to bless others through us.

So get your priorities in line. Establish a clear-cut goal. See your body as being completely healed. See your business grow. See your family joyful and happy. You can see these things when you pray for them. You're speaking the language of the Spirit when you do that. It is then when you will truly pray with faith. That's when a creative command will come, and it may surprise you when it does.

Such prayer brings the spiritual realm into the natural realm as if it's an already-done deal. It's over. It's done. In Jesus' name. Boom!

JACOB'S DREAM IS FULFILLED

Jacob worked hard for 20 years, and yet he was a poor man. Indeed, he had worked very hard and had nothing to show for it. And his strongest desire was, "I've got to get out of here! I've got to take my family away from this wicked Laban. And, God, I want to be a rich man. I want to own the most cattle, the most sheep. I'm tired of being a poor man."

God heard his prayer and knew the desire of Jacob's heart, so He gave him a revelation through a dream. As a result, Jacob told Laban, "Hey, I'll continue to work for you if you do one thing: I want you and your sons to take all the speckled and spotted sheep from the herds and give the all-black and all-white ones to me."

That ancient culture regarded the speckled and spotted sheep to be the very best premium sheep. The absolute best. The Bible then tells us (see Genesis 31) that Jacob developed a burning desire to have a vast number of animals. He told his uncle that in the future all the spotted and speckled sheep that would be born through his all-white or all-black sheep would stay with him.

Laban said, "Boy! This is a good deal. I'm getting all the spotted and speckled sheep. He's taking all the single-colored sheep." All the while Laban's thinking, "Hey, white sheep produce white sheep, and black sheep produce black sheep. Oh, once in a while a speckled one will come through. Once in a while, a hybrid will appear." So the two men made a deal, and Laban was happy with it.

Jacob then went to the mountain and got some chestnut trees and poplar trees. Then he carved the outer layers of wood from these, put poles up at every watering hole, at every trough where his single-colored sheep were drinking.

He knew that the sheep would mate at the watering troughs, and what did the animals see at that location? A spotted and speckled pole. As they are looking at the spotted and speckled pole and mating, Jacob begins to see and pray God's will for his harvest; he saw in his dreams that the pregnant she-lambs and she-goats would be filled with spotted and speckled goats and sheep. And guess what? They started giving birth to spotted and speckled sheep!

The newly born spotted and speckled sheep grew so numerous, in fact, that Laban said, "Hey, you've got to get out of here!" Thereby Jacob became the richest man in the Middle East, and this was because he spoke the language of the Spirit. He kept a clear-cut goal in his mind and his imagination.

He prayed, "God, I want to get out of here. And I want to get out of here and help my family more than anybody ever could. I want to be a rich man, Lord." God heard and answered his prayer. Jacob had a burning desire, and he had a plan that was connected to it, a plan that would ultimately bless his family.

When you have that desire in your heart for both your immediate family and your church family, God will start to move in your life. Jacob dreamed. He imagined. And stuff began to happen. Remember, it shall be done to you according to your faith.

Do you realize that the cross of Jesus Christ is spotted and it is speckled with blood? It is His own blood. And when you look at that Cross, it doesn't matter how poor you are, it doesn't matter what a failure you've been, or how nothing has ever seemed to work for you. When you look at that Cross, you're seeing the spotted and speckled pole of God crying out to all of you, that Jesus Christ is Lord over your body, over your healing, over your salvation, over your finances. He became sin for us who knew no sin, that we might be made the righteousness of God through Him. (See 2 Corinthians 5:21.)

This is our Lord, mighty and strong in battle, and yet He went to a thief's cross and died a sinner's death for you and for me, even though His life was impeccable. He was the Perfect One. He was the High and Lifted Up One. He came to earth and gave Himself freely. He surrendered His life, that you and I could receive salvation. Because of Him we can have every one of our sins forgiven, access to healing and protection in our lives, and deliverance from every addiction.

It's important to realize, also, that because of His obedience, the blessing of Jesus could come to our lives in financial ways, as well. Look on His Cross, and behold all that He has accomplished for you.

As You Believe, It Will Happen!

God has given me some wonderful mentors through the years. Oral Roberts taught me how to dream big. Dr. Ern Baxter taught me how the Church was going to accomplish all that Jesus and the Word said we would. No matter what circumstances develop in the earth, believe what God said in His Word concerning His Church. As you believe, it will happen.

Another one of my mentors, Dr. David Yonggi Cho, appeared in our lives. This skinny, little Korean preacher, who had nothing in the 1950s, was apprehended by God, who told him, "You're going to build a great church." In obedience, Dr. Cho put a little tent up. This happened after World War II. For months he had only five people attending services in the little tent, and one of these was his girlfriend!

Nonetheless, he preached loudly and intensely, causing his girlfriend to ask him, "Why are you preaching so loud? You're hurting our ears!"

Dr. Cho answered, "Because I'm not preaching only to you five. I'm preaching to the 300 that I see." Finally, after two years, the 300 started coming. Then Dr. Cho said, "God, I'm not happy with just 300. Let's go to 3,000. Then he went to 50,000, 100,000, 200,000, and more!

When I was with this dynamic man, his church numbered at around 200,000 people. He said, "I'm going to half a million!" Then, when they got to half a million, he took a long vacation with his dear wife. While he was away, he said, "Lord, we accomplished it. Now, I'm going to retire. I want to spend a lot of time golfing, and going to other countries."

The Holy Spirit responded, *"No you don't. We're going to a million!"* Now the church ministers to over a million people through satellite churches, and Dr. Cho has 750,000 in his Seoul, Korea, congregation. This great leader told me, "I've had thousands of poverty-stricken Koreans come who are millionaires today, because they looked at the Cross and they saw the spotted and speckled blood of Jesus Christ, and they prayed and imagined until their prayers became prayers of faith."

This same thing can happen to you! You are not exempt from the mighty blessings of God. He is the same, yesterday, today and forever more. (See Hebrews 13:8.) The blood of Jesus cries out victory in and for our lives. The Cross is our foundation, and there's nothing boring about praying with faith and imagination. The truth is that most people don't like prayer because they find it boring. This is because they don't expect any answers. Consequently they just utter ho-hum prayers, which I call "lottery prayers." They think, "I know my prayer is just one in how many; maybe three hundred million people are praying today in America." So they go to God and say, "Here's one of them, God; maybe you could hear it for me." There's no faith in that kind of prayer.

However, when you've dreamed and imagined what you're praying for, and you've prayed the Holy Spirit to send His fire upon it, and the desire to see it fulfilled is in your heart, and your goal is clear, the time will come when you are able to say, "Lord, I thank you. I've seen this thing with the eyes of my imagination, and I now know it's coming to pass." That prayer leaves the realm of simply believing and enters the realm of certain knowledge. Now imagine that!

CHAPTER 3

It's Time to Push the FM Button

Many Americans feel they have no control anymore. Because they have lost so much control of their lives and the way things are going in the world, they no longer get excited about possibilities that could really change them and their circumstances. Therefore, they "stay in their tents." In other words, they remain in mediocrity and maintain the status quo. Yet, once in a while they may allow themselves to dream.

As mentioned in the previous chapter, God said to Abraham, "I want to show you something." Then He took him outside into the night and said, "Look at the stars in the sky, because as many stars as there are in the sky is the size of the harvest of offspring you will have. They will bring My purposes to pass." Abraham could see the stars and he remembered God's word. So, every night when he saw the stars, he was able to speak the language of God in his dreams and in the visions he experienced.

We also looked at Jacob and saw how he had been a "failure" for 20 years. After those two decades passed, he developed a strong goal for his life: "I want to get out of poverty. I am tired of having no control in my life. I want to make wealth." These positive thoughts become his burning goals. God honored these goals, as He gave Jacob revelation concerning the spotted and speckled poles. As a result, Jacob moved out of poverty and became the richest man in the Middle East.

GOD'S LAWS WORK

The Bible shows us that His laws really do work. Your harvest comes to pass as you learn to pray in faith. We read about "the law of faith" in Romans 3:27. Like electricity, the law of faith is powerful.

As you know, we're living in what many call "the electronic age." I listened to radio broadcasts during Hurricane Katrina in which news people were saying, "There are two or three million people in southern Florida who are without power." In our modern age it's very challenging to be without electricity. It's much the same in the spiritual life; if you don't have electricity flowing in your spirit, you're without power. Similarly, if you don't have faith operating in your life, you are completely without power.

The loss of power is a terrible thing. People can't cook, shower, watch television, listen to radio, or even turn on lights. All electrical appliances are useless. It is similar in the Christian's life when there is a loss of spiritual power. The believer has nothing with which to defend himself from the world, the devil, and sin.

Someone might say, "I know all about the scriptural promises, but I have no power." How would you respond to such a statement? Would you tell that person that the way to get empowered is to get "hooked up" and "plugged into" God's supernatural world? There simply is no other way.

What do I mean by "God's supernatural world"? It is all around us. Someone might ask, "Is Heaven a place?" Yes it is, in the same way that Nairobi is a place and New York City is a place. But Heaven is a very special place, because it exists above and it exists within our spirits.

God is a Spirit. And if we're going to contact God, we have to learn the laws that govern the ability to contact Him. We are so sense-oriented that we always think we have to see, taste, hear, feel, or touch something for it to be real; but in the realm of the spirit, there is a different means of contact. It does not involve the five physical senses at all.

Did you know that within your house and neighborhood there are all kinds of signals filling the air? These include UHF, VHF, satellite, radio waves, cellular signals, etc. In what ways do you connect with these waves of energy? Literally, there's music in the air. The signal is right where you are. Waves of music are all around you. Because you can't hear them or see them, does not mean that they don't exist, however. In order to receive them and perceive them, you need to activate the connections. But how do you plug in? In order to do so you must get a receiver and use it properly.

When you get your receiver, you are able to receive the signal, and suddenly that which you can't see, will become something you actually hear. Amazing, isn't it? What was invisible and inaudible can now be heard. There are things that I can't see that are real—more real, in fact, than the things I do see!

UNDERSTANDING BY FAITH

In Hebrews 11:3 we learn that the worlds were framed by the Word of God. This helps us to realize that the things which we are able to see were made by things we cannot see. Therefore, the things which are seen were not made of things which are visible. The things we see are held together by invisible atoms and molecules.

In the same way that all these invisible electronic signals are being sent out all around us, God has His signals going forth in the spirit world. Our receiver for His signals is faith. When we grow in faith, we will be on "the receiving end" every day, and this will enable us to experience the comfort of the Holy Spirit and to receive His direction for our lives.

We must get illumination and revelation knowledge from God's Word, so that we will not be lost, floundering, and losing control in our lives. God has outlined a specific way for us to live. Paul writes, *"The just shall live by faith"* (Rom. 1:17). Who are "the just"? They are the ones whom God proclaims as being righteous.

He declares that, when you receive Jesus as your Lord and Savior, you are righteous. When we come to the Lord to live our life in faith, we are given a supernatural ability to receive things from Him by faith. As a result, we know where we're going and we know also that we are equipped for the journey. Likewise, we realize that we're never at a loss and no matter what valley or obstacle we may have to face, we know we can always get through it or overcome it, because we're living by faith. Don't count yourself out. The just shall live by faith. Remember, you are justified, which means God sees you just as if you had never sinned because of Jesus' blood in your life.

How Faith Works

In James 1 we see how vital it is to understand how faith works and how it brings us into a brand-new place of blessing. James writes, *"My brethren, count it all joy when you fall into various trials* [or temptations or tests]" (James 1:2).

What is the purpose of a test? It serves to prove how much knowledge you have. The amount of knowledge you have determines whether or not you can pass any given test. The devil will throw tests at you to see whether or not you're living in faith or just floating along in a doubting lifestyle with a little bit of wishing here and there. The devil is able to defeat us through simple things like losing control or thinking, "It doesn't matter what I do anymore, the deck is stacked against me."

God says, *"Count it all joy when you fall into various trials* [tests], *knowing that the testing of your faith produces patience* [endurance]. *But let patience* [endurance] *have its perfect work, that you may be complete, lacking nothing"* (James 1:2-4).

Wouldn't it be wonderful if we could reach a place in God where we know that we lack nothing? A place where we know we have everything we need? A place where we know we have access to everything? God enables us to receive everything we need from His spirit realm, for He is Spirit. Through the Spirit, therefore, we are able to bring everything we need into the "nowness" of our lives.

Jesus told us that the Kingdom of Heaven is near us. In fact, He said, *"...The kingdom of God is within you"* (Luke 17:21).

Yes, the Kingdom of Heaven a place. One day we'll be going to this special place. But we don't have to wait till then, because it's also a spirit place in the here-and-now of our lives. It's right here. God has not left us without His Presence and His witness. All we need is to know that our "receiver" is working.

We "turn on" our receiver of faith, and we know that Jesus is right there with us. The Holy Spirit is right there, as well. The Comforter is right there, and your Director's right there. Your Elder Brother is right there with you, and He will defeat the enemy and quench the fiery darts that come against you.

FM—THE FAITH MODE

So, turn the dial on your receiver from AM to FM. By FM I mean "the Faith Mode." Get positive about it. Say, "I am going to start my walk. I'm going to get belief into me."

You see, there are many people who have accepted Jesus, have had their sins forgiven, and know that their home is in Heaven and yet they are living a miserable life! Why does this sometimes happen? It's because they haven't learned to use their "receivers"!

God doesn't want that for you, and I don't want that for you either. You should be enjoying life as one of the happiest people on earth. God is there with you, to help you with His grace. Jesus is the Lord, but in order to make His Lordship a reality in your life, you must be able to say, "I'm believing this truth in my heart now." You bring it out of the realm of weak belief into faith by confessing it, and you confess the truth with your tongue. Make this declaration: "Jesus Christ is my Lord and Savior; He died for me and rose again for me and at that moment God took me out of darkness into His marvelous light. I've been born again, and I am a new creation!" (See Romans 10:9 and 2 Corinthians 5:17.)

All too often people choose to live in the old creation, and because this is true, they never approach anything extraordinary in their lives. Paul told us not to act like "mere men." Why did he choose these words? I believe it's because when we accept Jesus, we have within us a whole new DNA code. God takes a part of Himself and puts it within us!

HARVEST YOUR DREAMS

Read Acts 2, which tells us what God is going to do in our day—the last days, which, by the way, started on the Day of Pentecost. You don't need to be waiting around for Jesus. He wants you to "occupy until He comes." In Acts 2:17 we read, *"And it shall come to pass in the last days,' says God, that I will pour out of My Spirit on all flesh...."*

Remember, Peter was telling the believers what they were seeing and experiencing as they were receiving the Holy Spirit. He explained to them, that what they were experiencing had been foretold by the Prophet Joel. He quoted Joel's prophecy: *"And it shall come to pass in the last days, says God, that I will pour out of My Spirit on all flesh..."* (Joel 2:28).

Do you realize that God is putting a part of Himself in you. He's pouring out of His Spirit on your flesh. Your sons and daughters shall prophesy; they will boldly proclaim the Word of God. This passage is not talking about predicted future things only. Instead, it's proclaiming that we can talk boldly, and in faith we can command things through the Word of God!

Joel wrote, "*Your young men shall see visions*" (see Joel 2:28 and Acts 2:17). In other words, they'll be able to see things that other people aren't seeing. He goes on, "*Your old men shall dream dreams*." Did you know that it's through your imagination that you are able to harvest your dreams?

Begin now. Harvest your dreams through your imagination. This is so vital in this time when so many people believe they have lost control. Many Americans and people around the world feel trapped.

The well-known editor and writer Norman Cousins was told by the medical profession that he was going to die and that he should go home and "put his things in order" in preparation for his departure from this life. Instead of heeding their advice, he went into the hospital and took some interesting things with him: some Marx Brothers and Laurel and Hardy movie clips along with other comedies. He came out of the hospital laughing; and he lived a long time afterward. He said, "Progress is possible only when people believe in the possibilities of growth and change."

Races and tribes die out when they accept their losses as ultimate defeat, become despairing, and lose their excitement about the future. The Church has lost its excitement about the future of the glory of God covering this planet. Ninety percent of Christendom is just waiting to "get out of here." Jesus never told us that we should be waiting to "get out of here." Instead, He told us to go to everyone and tell them about a new life and a new lifestyle.

Today, though, many Americans have a fear of terrorism, loss of finances, crime, and many other things. They feel victimized by industries that are outsourcing and cutting payrolls. We used to think that we were number one in health. Now, though, the United States has become number 11 in the world! An infant in the United States has more chance of dying during birth in the hospital during its first three days of life, than babies in ten other countries do.

The truth is that the United States is no longer number one in many things. People now are working on an average of 49 hours a week instead of just 41 hours a week, which was the average a few years ago. Now there are two working parents in nearly every family, and people still feel trapped. We need a new heart and new eyes to see that we can generate new solutions to the problems in the world; we need to rise above the attitude that says, "It doesn't matter anymore."

THE "SHOCKED RAT SYNDROME"

In a recent experiment, researchers took two rats and put them in separate cages. These scientists had electric current wired up in such a way that when a rat pressed a button, the current would go through both cages. A lever that was designed to stop the electric current had been placed in only one of the cages, however. When the rat that was in the cage with the lever hit it, the electric shock stopped in both cages.

The researchers would press the button, releasing electrical current to the cages, and the rats in both cages would start running frantically all over the place, sniffing, going crazy, and trying to find out what they could do to protect themselves from the shock. The rat, which was in the cage with the lever, happened to knock against it by accident and thereby discovered the way to stop the flow of electricity to both cages.

That same rat soon learned how to regain his comfort in the cage. He knew that when he pressed the lever, the electric shock would cease. The researchers continued working with both of these rats, and they discovered that the rat in the cage with the lever had great learning ability and perseverance. When they put him in other difficult situations, he would always keep trying to find a way to overcome the problem. For example, he would never get lost in a maze.

The other rat, the one in the cage without the lever, had learned during the electric shock experiments, that there was nothing he could do about it, so he stopped running around and went into a corner and laid there despondently. Before long, that rat was no longer in a world of reality. When the scientists put that rat in other difficult experiments, he was completely lost. He simply didn't know what to do.

They'd open the cage, and even then, he wouldn't jump out! I believe that something similar has taken place in America. So many people feel trapped, and quite a few Christians are even experiencing depression. God does not want us to be passive. He wants us to be involved in doing what we can to help others and to effect positive changes in our world. He poured out of His own Spirit so we would be empowered. His Spirit is within us, and He wants us to be active agents of His new creation. This is our mission, and to accomplish it we must grow in faith and understand what it means to come to actually move in the Spirit so as to actually change circumstances and conditions.

Studies have also been conducted on chimpanzees.[1] In every tribal situation concerning these chimps, there is one male leader, often the biggest one in the pack. This "chieftain" walks upright, has a confident gait, enjoys life, makes all the other chimps serve him, and he gets the first pick of all the females. The other males stoop their shoulders more and eventually they experience less of a sex drive, due to the fact that they are sometimes beaten by the leader when they try to get one of the females. They even begin to stoop over and lose some of their muscles.

There are even examples of some male chimpanzees whose muscles keep degenerating until the leader dies or is destroyed by another tribe. Those same weaker chimps were trying to make it through life, but they were despairing and despondent because they thought they were and always would be the "have-nots." However, when the leader succumbed, these other male chimps were suddenly energized, and they begin competing for the top male position.

Researchers say that during this period of competition the physiology of these male chimps actually changes. Their postures get straighter. Their sex drive comes back. They get excited about life again. They look for new things, and they become experimental in their attitude toward life.

The same thing happens to people. When you feel there is really little difference you can make and you don't have control over anything, then you're going to stoop over and you're not going to be excited about finding new solutions to the problems of your life. The wells of creativity and enthusiasm in your life dry up. You won't even be excited about a meeting with mentors, and you definitely won't be excited about meeting with a motivator or somebody else who learned how to have major breakthroughs in life.

In all probability you'll say, "I've heard it before. I don't really have any control over my own life." Then you'll talk yourself into being despondent. You'll lay in the corner of the cage, waiting for retirement some day. Let me assure you of one thing—retirement will only kill you! Do you understand that? Retirement will put you in a sleepy, passive state, and this is not what God wants for you.

During the French Revolution, officials conducted an experiment with a man who was sentenced to die by the guillotine[2]. In effect, they said, "Look, we're not going to send you to the guillotine, which is a horrible way to die. We're going to make your death a little 'easier.' You won't have to have your head chopped off after all. Here's what we propose: One of these days we'll come into your cell and blindfold you, and then we will slit your wrist. All you will have to do then is just lie down and die. You'll feel the blood ooze out, but it will be a kind of peaceful death." They told this to the man over and over again. Then he started to imagine it, and to envision what this scenario would actually be like.

As an experiment, one day they went into his cell, blindfolded the man, took a sharp piece of ice, and began pretending to cut his wrist. They also had some kind of red ointment that looked like blood, and they let it run down his arm.

Next they laid him down in the cell. Within 20 minutes, he was dead! What killed him? His death came to him not from any kind of fatal torture or execution; his death came from his own mind, his imagination!

LOVE AND WORSHIP GOD WITH YOUR IMAGINATION

Jesus said, "*You shall love the Lord your God with all your heart, with all your soul, and with all your mind*" (Matt.

22:37). Heart, soul, and mind. Now follow me in this. Your heart connects your spirit and your soul. Your soul is that place in your mind where your will, your intellect, and your emotions reside. It's the place where you sense things.

The word for "mind" in this verse is a Greek word, *dianoia*, which means "imagination." Therefore, Jesus was actually saying, "I want you to love Me, not just with your intellect, your emotions, and your willpower, and your heart, but I want you to love Me with your *imagination*."

God has given us a creative capacity within our minds. And that creative part involves the language the Holy Spirit uses. He has made us to be rational people, and we don't want to do away with our sense of reason. It's very useful to us. For example, when I'm about to cross to the road, and I see a big Mack truck coming, I will probably think very quickly, "Steel against flesh! All right. A big, powerful truck and little me! I'm not stupid, so I'm not going to walk out there and let that Mack truck hit me!" Thank God for our ability to reason and use common sense.

I worship God with my soul, my rational being. But I also worship God with my *dianoia*. As you know, Jesus said, "*... You shall not commit adultery. But I say to you that everyone who looks at a woman to lust after her has committed adultery in his heart*" (Matt. 5:27-28). The Greek word that is translated as "heart" in this passage is cardia, and it means "the thoughts or feelings of the mind."

Notice that Jesus, through this warning, is pointing to a picture in the mind. What is your mind thinking? What is your mind seeing? Jesus said that when you begin to see something, really see it in your mind, it's the same as if it has actually happened or is taking place. When you see yourself, with your mind's eye, as being involved in any act, it's as if you've already committed the thing you're envisioning. Now why did He say that? It's because Jesus knew the laws of the spirit realm—that if you see something long enough in your imagination, it's going to get down into your heart and eventually it will manifest in your life.

Mental pictures will continue to grow, and what you dwell upon in your mind and imagination will eventually become behavior in your life. In other words, what you see, you're eventually going to receive.

VAIN IMAGINATIONS

The Bible says, "*Because, although they knew God, they did not glorify Him as God, nor were thankful, but became futile in their thoughts* [vain in their imaginations], *and their foolish hearts were darkened*" (Rom. 1:21).

The unthankful idolaters mentioned here became *vain in their imaginations*. We see this in the world today; there's vainness in people's imaginations right now in the world, and their imaginations are often used for evil.

Jesus said that He wanted to turn around that tendency toward vain imaginations. The truth is that He wants to have a new day among His people. He wants to pour out of His Spirit into our lives so we will begin to experience the fullness of His life on a daily basis. Part of this will happen through visions and dreams. As I said before, this doesn't mean that you will become spooky.

Rather, it becomes a beautiful part of your life and your prayer life. It's so vital for you to understand this. Too many people always dwell on the negative, but we've got to become positive and to see the positive truths of this important teaching.

The story of the Tower of Babel speaks to this. Read Genesis 11. The people depicted in this chapter were all beginning to say the same thing, because they had seen the same thing—world rulership outside of God's will. The Bible says, *"And the Lord said, 'Indeed the people are one and they all have one language, and this is what they begin to do; now nothing that they propose to do will be withheld from them...'"* (Gen. 11:6). God is saying here that nothing will be able to stop these people from doing what they have imagined. The word propose is *yetser* and it means "imagination" in the Hebrew language. Some translations even substitute imagination for the word propose, and it is equivalent to the Greek word, *dianoia.*

God is saying that the imagination is so powerful that, when people are in unity with it, and they're all seeing the same thing, they will begin to say the same thing. As a result, this spiritual law will work for them, as it will for anybody else. As you can see this spiritual law will work for evil as well as for good.

One look into the realm of evil shows us that this is true. Look at what the world is doing when people work in organization with each other, even though they are outside of God's will. They get organized by setting clear-cut goals; and we must do the same. They visualize success, and we must do the same.

Unfortunately, we've allowed the world to take our principles, which were given to us by God, and use them against us. This happens because we're "waiting to get out," and we're feeling as if we have no control over anything. We too quickly forget what God told us in His Word: *"And the Lord will make you the head and not the tail; you shall be above only, and not be beneath, if you heed the commandments of the Lord your God"* (Deut. 28:13).

The glory of the Lord is going to cover the entire the earth like the waters cover the sea, and you're among the people who will see this take place, the people who are more than conquerors. In light of these facts of our faith, why have so many already forfeited the game? Let's play to win, and we shall be victorious!

One day in 1987, we ran out of the money needed for the building of our church. The church treasurer told me, "We're going to have to let the workers go, because we don't have enough money to pay them next week. We're going to have to let them go on Friday."

We never had to do such a thing before. We always had enough money to pay everybody for what they did. I responded by going to prayer. When I prayed, I saw a pile of money as high as the church dome, which then was just a wooden framework. It was a 40-foot-high wooden structure, and that's all it was. The builders were working hard. In my spirit I saw money piled up as high as the dome—40 feet high!

My friend John Avanzini called me around this same time. He said, "You know, I had a thought. To complete all the vision God has given for that area, you're going to need money the size of that dome." When he said those words, something clicked in me. My imagination was ignited!

I said, "Ah. I saw it, and I believe." God was confirming His word to me, so I began to pray throughout the next two days. Every time I prayed, I saw a mountain of cash that went all the way to the top of the dome! It wasn't long before a businessman called me and took me out to lunch. This happened on a Wednesday, just a few days after the church treasurer had made his dire prediction.

The businessman said, "Listen, this church has transformed my life. Since I 'got in' on these principles from the Word, God has really blessed my finances. I've been following those principles consistently, and some great things are happening in my life." Then he said, "I want to share this with you," and he handed me a $30,000 check! As he placed the check in my hand, he said, "And next week I'm bringing you another check, and that one will be written out in the amount of $34,000!"

Rejoicing in my heart over God's faithfulness, I ran back to the building site and said, "Hey, workers, don't go anywhere!" We were able to finish the project with excellence, thanks to this man's obedience to God, who had made a trustworthy promise to me.

I think it's very important to remember, though, that I first saw it before I could receive it. This took place in the spirit realm—the FM realm. Just tune in and see your future. Now imagine that!

Endnotes

1. Howard Bloom, *The Lucifer Principle* (New York, 1999), 197.

2. Col. Stringer, *The Eyes of Your Understanding* (Australia, 1990), tape.

CHAPTER 4

The Piano Man—Developing
Your Creativity

I have discovered that developing your personal creativity can be a fun-filled adventure. Paul writes, *"Therefore I also, after I heard of your faith in the Lord Jesus and your love for all the saints, do not cease to give thanks for you, making mention of you in my prayers: that the God of our Lord Jesus Christ, the Father of glory, may give to you the spirit of wisdom and revelation in the knowledge of Him"* (Eph. 1:15-17).

The word "revelation" here has a little prefix in the Greek: *epi,* which means "super." The prefix is followed by *gnosis,* which means "revelation knowledge." Therefore, Paul is talking about super-revelation knowledge here, not just some ordinary revelation, but *super* revelation.

He goes on with his prayer: *"...the eyes of your understanding being enlightened; that you may know what is the hope of His calling, what are the riches of the glory of His inheritance in the saints, and what is the exceeding greatness of His power toward us who believe according to the working of His mighty power which He worked in Christ when He raised Him from the dead and seated Him at His right hand in heavenly places, far above all principality and power and might and dominion, and every name that is named, not only in this age but also in that which is to come. And He put all things under His feet, and gave Him to be head over all things to the church, which is His body, the fullness of Him who fills all in all"* (Eph. 18-23).

Notice how this passage says that *His body, the Church,* is the fullness of Him. We've not yet entered into the full understanding of this truth. There is so much more!

YOUR TURNING POINT

Right now a holy hush may come over your mind as you endeavor to control your thoughts and realize that this truly is a special time for you. This is a turning point for your life, because you can turn toward that which is going to fulfill you and bring life to you, providing you with a whole, new purpose and a fulfilled destiny. This is a great moment in which to have a major perspective change. I want you, my reader, to do exactly what you have been called to do and have fun doing it. You will see that in doing so you will become contagious and others will want what you have.

In the late 1960s there was a man who had a dream. He became a famous musician. He knew exactly what he wanted to do, so he left high school in order to pursue his dream. At that time he did not feel that high school could really help him achieve the fulfillment of his dream.

When many people drop out of high school, a downward spiral begins in their lives; however, in some people's lives, when they drop out of college or high school, it's because they know exactly how to take a step up. At this point in their lives they begin to move toward something that everything inside screams, "This is it!"

This seemed to be the case with the man I just mentioned. However, it was really rough for him, and he had a very difficult time after he left school. He started performing in small clubs and bars, and he grew weary and discouraged as he sang for a handful of drunks. He had dreamed of performing for sell-out crowds nationwide and around the world. He had dreamed of seeing his name up in lights and down the streets. He could see people lined up to get his autograph. These were the things he had imagined for himself.

He dreamed that his albums were in every music store in America and around the world. He even imagined that one day he would perform for a packed-out baseball stadium audience. But life got tough and it looked like things weren't getting any better for him. Before long, he was totally broke, and the only joy in his life was a girlfriend who had supported him.

The two of them started to spend their nights in 24-hour laundromats in order to save money. When his girlfriend grew weary of this gypsy lifestyle, she finally left him. After she left, he decided to commit suicide because he thought he had lost his only joy in life.

On the night when he decided to commit suicide, this young singer and songwriter drank a bottle of shoe polish and a bottle of vodka. He woke up the next day, however, to discover that he wasn't dead, but he was very sick. At this point he checked himself into a mental hospital.

Less than three weeks later, he released himself from the hospital. When he checked out, he knew he was a new man. He felt refreshed, excited, rested, and was ready for life once again. His recovery didn't come through the staff in that hospital. He said that the other patients "cured" him. How did they do so? They reminded him of how blessed and gifted he was.

He now felt that he had been given a second chance, a new opportunity. On the day when he left the mental institution, he determined that he was going to travel. He made up his mind that he would work and do whatever was necessary to see that his dream would come true. Three years later he wrote a song.

Today, people all over the world know him. His dream was fulfilled, and on June 22 and 23 in 1990, he performed the song he wrote to a sell-out crowd of 90,000 people at Yankee Stadium in New York. He has become known as the "piano man," and his name is Billy Joel. He was and is a man with a dream, a man who wasn't afraid to use his imagination. His dream came true even though he had tried to kill himself and had checked himself into a mental institution. Those early brushes with death and insanity changed his destiny.[1] Sometimes in life all of us need a startling, new perspective. Billy Joel certainly needed one, and it came as mental patients reminded him of how blessed he was. He then imagined, and what he imagined came true.

Through this example I want to show you how important your imagination is. I want you to know that the Bible has a lot to say about the power of your imagination. There's a great danger in our lives that we will just see ourselves as we are right now. In so doing we may think that nothing will ever change. The truth is that there is always more to life than what you are seeing and experiencing right now.

Therefore, you need to ask yourself, "Do I really know that there's more to life than this?" You are not stuck. You are able to move on.

When was the last time you saw a news program or talk show on television? In all likelihood, the program presented an expert in some field. It seems as if we're allowing our lives to be governed by the opinions of too many people who claim they're experts in certain fields, but we must remember that they're not necessarily experts in caring for you and me.

Many experts will tell you something that will make you dependent on them, their system, their books, or some other thing. When we listen to them, we may feel as if we're being batted around like a ping-pong ball as we listen first to one expert and then another.

Some people even go so far as to surrender their lives to these experts, whether the experts be doctors, priests, politicians, scientists, writers, or teachers. We may even surrender our lives to our pastor, priest, or teacher. Now, please don't get me wrong. It certainly isn't wrong to learn from and respect our teachers, but all too frequently we accept their advice without question and find out later that they were wrong and our intuition was right. Has this ever happened to you?

SEEING INTO THE INVISIBLE

The Bible says, "*While we do not look at the things which are seen, but at the things which are not seen. For the things which are seen are temporary, but the things which are not seen are eternal*" (2 Cor. 4:18). How do we look at things that we cannot see? You have to do it within the realm of your imagination.

That's how God works, and He wants us to become like Him.

Paul writes, "*God...calls those things which do not exist as though they did*" (Rom. 4:17). That's how God operates. God calls those things that aren't as though they are. It is by faith, not by sight, that we understand that God framed the world by his Word. (See Hebrews 11:3.)

Through the windows of our imagination we are able to perceive many spiritual truths. I wonder why we haven't heard more teaching about this? Why aren't there more books written on this important topic? It's because the forces of darkness, satan and his hordes, do not want this enlightening and liberating truth released in people's lives. He wants people to remain confused, bewildered, discouraged, and defeated.

We know that the left side of our brain is the side where logic and language develop, and the right hemisphere houses our creative faculties. Many people major on the left side of their brains and leave the right side—the place where your imagination resides—relatively undeveloped.

I believe this is why Paul prays that, "*...the eyes of your understanding* [your heart] *being enlightened...*" (Eph. 1:18). Have you ever seen a person wearing eyeglasses over his or her chest? What does the apostle mean by "the eyes of your heart"? He's talking about your understanding and your imagination (*dianoia*—the Greek word that is used here for "heart" or "understanding"). When this happens, we will begin to perceive who we are and the great abilities and possibilities that are within us.

In Mark 5, we see Jesus and another person who is pulling on His heart. This sick woman is getting Jesus' attention, because she wants Him to heal her of the hemorrhaging she has suffered for 12 years. In Mark 5:25-28, we see this woman putting a demand on Jesus. The Bible says, *"Now a certain woman had a flow of blood for twelve years, and she had suffered many things from many physicians. She had spent all that she had and was no better, but rather grew worse"* (Mark 5:25-26).

Take a good look at what happened next: *"When she heard about Jesus, she came behind Him in the crowd and touched His garment"* (Mark 5:27). The garment Jesus was wearing was a robe with tassels along the bottom seam. These tassels represented God's covenant. They were the covenant part of the priestly robe. The lady touched the hem of His garment where the tassels were. In other words, she touched His covenant—His law of life for you and me.

She said, *"If only I may touch His clothes, I shall be made well"* (Mark 5:28). Why did she make this statement of faith? Obviously she had been doing a lot of praying and thinking. She had spent all her money on doctors who caused her to suffer many things, but the hemorrhage continued. No doubt she heard about Jesus at some point and how He could change her life and heal her. She must have thought, "I've got to meet Him. I've got to find this man somewhere."

When she learned about His whereabouts, she kept repeating, "If only I may touch his clothes, I shall be made well." She said this over and over again (see Mark 5:28 AMP). What is she doing here? She's picturing her healing in her mind. She's using her imagination to secure her healing. To her, touching the hem of the Master's garment was the all-important thing. She knew she had to do it even thought it was hard to get through the crowd to Him. Perhaps she was even knocked to the ground. Nonetheless, she finally found Him, and she reached out in faith and touched His garment.

When this happened, Jesus said, "*Who touched My clothes?*" (Mark 5:30). He knew that someone had touched Him, because He felt power and virtue flowing from Him. Jesus' disciples asked, "What do you mean?" They saw the throngs around Jesus and thought it was silly to ask such a question. But Jesus knew what had happened.

Sometimes we can get overly familiar with those who represent the Lord, and thereby we miss out on the miracle. This lady, however, reached out and stretched herself so as to grasp the covenant tassel on Jesus' robe, and the Master said, "*Daughter, your faith has made you well. Go in peace, and be healed of your affliction*" (Mark 5:34).

She had entered a new place in her life because she had heard something that opened the windows of her imagination and stirred her faith, and she set that as her goal. She began to pray, and in her praying she began to confess her healing and to see it with the eyes of her spirit. Her heart's cry was, "*If I can just touch Him, or even just touch His clothes, I'll be made whole*" (Mark 5:28). She acted upon her faith and then she received. When she touched what she had imagined, His clothes, the healing virtue and power of Jesus, the Great Physician, ran throughout her body and the flow of blood that had plagued her for so long completely stopped.

ONE PICTURE IS WORTH A THOUSAND WORDS

Peter writes, "*Therefore gird up the loins of your mind*" (1 Pet. 1:13). The loins of the mind are the realm of the *dianoia*, your imagination. To gird them up is to bind them about with constant repetition. This is something you constantly do. It becomes a way of life. You imagine it. You see a picture of it happening. And then you speak that picture forth and it creates and reproduces what you see. Something always begins to happen when you do this!

I know this is true because we used this principle in our planning and building of the Shore Christian Center facilities. We saw it, we dreamed it, we envisioned it, we heard the basketballs bouncing on the court in our minds, and we saw the children in their classes. All of these wonderful things began in the reproductive side of our minds, as we used our imagination (*dianoia*) before anything was even built.

You pray it, and then you speak the language of the Spirit in your imagination. You picture what you want in your mind. That is the specific word of God to you.

How do we have communion and fellowship with the Holy Spirit? If we're going to commune with Him, we have to learn to speak His language. A lot of people say, "Well, if I speak in tongues, that's His language, isn't it?" Yes, but that's not all there is. When the Holy Spirit comes, you're going to see visions and you're going to dream dreams. These dreams and visions are stirred by the Holy Spirit in the realm of your imagination.

You can have dreams like those that Billy Joel dreamed. No matter how far down and out you are, even if you're in a mental institution, you can come out of that situation and go on to see Yankee Stadium filled or whatever your dream might be. Do you understand the truth and power that are inherent in seeing a picture of what you want with your imagination?

I'm sure there are thousands of people who are playing the piano in bars and honky tonks today that just aren't able to go on to higher aspirations because they got stuck where they are. In his song, "Piano Man," Joel sings, "I just want to get out of here." He is singing about what he was thinking when he was stuck in a situation he didn't like. But he didn't let himself down. And you mustn't let yourself down either. He did not remain stuck, and you do not need to stay stuck either.

PERFECT PEACE

Isaiah writes, "*You will keep him in perfect peace, whose mind is stayed on You, because he trusts in You*" (Isa. 25:3). As mentioned previously, the word "mind" that is used in this verse is from the Hebrew word *yetser*, which refers to the creative side of our minds (our imagination—*dianoia*). This Hebrew term entails "conceiving," and it literally means "the thing framed." *Yetser* is the imagination, and it means "work" as well as "mind."

You've got to do some work in your mind in order to imagine. This is a conceptual thing. What happens is this: Something is conceived on the inside of your mind, because you were born with a "womb" in your spirit. The left hemisphere of your mind is for relating and correlating information every day. The right side is where you get a picture of something. On the right side of your mind you hear a word from God, then you form a picture of it. From then on you begin to speak to yourself inside and out.

That's why the hemorrhaging woman kept saying to herself, "If I could only touch the hem of His garment." She heard about His power. She believed in His ability to heal her. She saw her healing in her mind, and she began speaking it to herself. You have to speak it for yourself, as she did. That's why we say *yetser* involves work. And sometimes it's hard work—the kind of labor that's involved with conception. All this takes place in the realm of your imagination. This is what God wants for your life so you will have good success and experience His perfect peace.

In Proverbs we read, *"For as he thinks in his heart, so is he"* (Prov. 23:7). This is biblical truth and it has been proven time and time again in the world. Whatever people think about themselves is what they become. Take a look at any other person. That person is a manifestation of what he or she is thinking or what they have thought throughout their lives. Sometimes you can tell what those thoughts are or were by just observing the person's facial expressions and body language.

Similarly, your future will become what you imagine it to be—right now. Do you understand the importance of this? Your future will be what you imagine right now. Billy Joel left the mental hospital. Nothing had changed, except his image of himself and his future. He said, "I'll do whatever it takes to fulfill my dream."

How is your *yetser* being formed? For many of us it's being formed by the print and broadcast media. It's also framed by family, friends, relatives, peers, coaches, and bosses. But God is saying, "*Would you let me frame that creative side of your mind by telling you who you really are?*"

Paul prayed that the eyes of our understanding [our heart, the eyes of our *heart*—our *dianoia*] would understand God's ways. (See Ephesians 1:18.) God has so much in store for each and every one of us who is in Christ. So what do you want in your life? Do you want what your boss says? What your coach says? What the media says? Or do you want a word from God? When you get a word from God, a picture will form in your imagination, and that picture, that image, will control your future.

I don't want my future controlled by forces that aren't able to see my great destiny and potential. So get a word from God. You get His word through prayer. Once you have it, start repeating it, and you put a picture with that word. Begin to listen to your own voice as you speak that word. Make sure, however, that the word you are speaking and the picture you are seeing are in line with the truths of God's Word.

The Bible tells us that King David looked over his balcony one day and he saw Bathsheba taking a bath. This happened at a time when the king should have been out with the troops on the front lines. It was a season of warfare. Instead, he stayed home after sending his soldiers out, and he began to watch a beautiful woman taking a bath. What he saw stirred the creative side of his mind—his *yetser*. The more he looked, the more he wanted to see. The longer he stayed there looking at her, the more something started to be conceived in the "womb" of his spirit. Eventually he saw himself actually engaged in an act of romance, passion, and sexual lust with

Bathsheba. Maybe that is the reason she was called Bathsheba!

We don't know how many days he looked at her, or how many hours. He probably knew when she would be bathing, though. As he watched, lust was conceived in his heart. The seed entered his mind, and it began to germinate, eventually giving birth to thing he saw. David played this scene over and over in his mind. This is what happens with lust. James writes, *"But each one is tempted when he is drawn away by his own desires and enticed. Then, when desire has conceived, it gives birth to sin..."* (James 1:14-15).

Your imagination is as real as the real thing, because it opens the door to the fulfillment of what it desires. Your imagination is a powerful tool, which can be used for good or evil in your life. Therefore, make sure that what you are imagining is lining up with God's will and His word for your life. Remember, the enemy is invading people's imaginations all the time.

About 12 years ago, I sat down with an Australian teacher, Cole Stringer. I asked him, "Cole, how did you become so successful in Australia? You have hundreds of churches."

He looked at me and said, "Mate, it's imagination."

I said, "Imagination?"

"Yes, imagination" Then this short, little man exemplified this point for me: "My wife and I had children, and all our kids were short little runts." He explained that this was characteristic of the family line. He went on, "My wife got tired of it. When she became pregnant with our last child, she began to pray every day, 'I'm going to have a six-foot-four son. I'm going to have a six-foot-four son."

Cole told me that she prayed this every day. "I thought she was crazy," he said. "Guess what," he continued, "My son's a policeman now; he's grown, and he's six-foot-four!"

Cole's wife set a goal, and she prayed earnestly and feverishly to bring it to birth. She engaged the spirit realm to help her see her dream come true. She saw it, she imagined it, and it happened.

We see this confirmed in world history, as well. The Spartans were a race of supermen. What did the Spartan fathers do? They carved statues of great, strong men with chiseled bodies and put them in their homes and yards, so their sons would see these figures and emulate them. They did something similar when their wives were pregnant; they placed beautiful figurines of shapely women in front of them. The result was that these Spartans gave birth to a generation of champions and giants in the world—men and women who were known for their strength, valor, and beauty.

This principle of visualization is something that the occult realm understands. It's also in the Bible, but many Christians run from it because the occult sciences use it. Though the Delphic Oracle of ancient Greece spoke in tongues does not mean that all speaking in tongues is from the devil. We see this today even with the symbol of a rainbow, which is used by the New Age Movement. This does not mean that we have to abandon its use, however.

Why should we neglect our God-given tools—our imaginations, our spiritual gifts, the rainbow, and visualization just because the world uses these things? I think there are "piano men" and "piano women" who are reading this book. You don't have to remain stuck where you are. There are people who have yet to crack the realm of God's blessing, people who will bring God's bounty to the Church of Jesus Christ so we all can be full. (See Ephesians 4.)

The French emperor Napoleon was a little, 5-foot-2-inch guy. He wrote that for five years before he ever went into battle he spent his time imagining victory. He said he imagined victory strategies that showed him how to win battles. As a result, it took three of the world's greatest armies to defeat this "little big man," who said, "Imagination rules the world."[2]

This thought was echoed by Albert Einstein who said, "Imagination is more important than knowledge."[3] You can make this power—the power of your imagination—work for you. Doing so actually makes prayer fun, because, as you begin to imagine and pray what God has given to you for you to use in your own life, you will begin to see it. Seeing it is the fun part. The more you see it in your imagination, the more you will begin to feel it.

As you see it and feel it, you can pray more earnestly about it. Then there will come a time when you know that you know that you know that it's going to happen because it's already happened. This truth is for the Church. It is for *you*. All you have to do is say yes to God. The Old Testament word *yetser* and New Testament word *dianoia* are both for you, and they are for your use on a daily basis.

Peter tells us to gird up the loins of our minds. You do so by beginning to see and to say your dream, until it becomes faith in you. Once the faith is there, the law of faith will bring forth fruit just as any natural law does. When we begin to envision our dream being fulfilled, something good always happens.

What about your family? Are your children lost? Do you still see them as being lost? What about your business ventures? Do you say, "I've never wanted anything, and this will fail too"? Such a negative confession will cause what you say to come to pass, because by saying it you've already framed your world for now and in the future.

Someone might say, "Oh, I can never lose weight." They are speaking the truth because that is what they see and believe. If you see yourself as being fat when you look in the mirror, you'll stay fat in the future. You have to start seeing yourself as the person you want to be. Even the greatest bodybuilders in the world understand this truth. The former Mr. South Africa, Ray McCauley, said, "When you're lifting and you're trying to change your body, it won't do much unless you concentrate with a mental picture." Basically, he is saying, "What you see is what you'll get."

I watch people in the gym who read books while they're working out. Some people sit on a bicycle while reading a book, or they do so while they're jogging on the treadmill. Other people will talk to their buddies while they are lifting weights. I believe this could actually distract them from seeing their dreams realized because it takes their minds off their goals. You have to envision the blood flowing into your muscles and the muscles growing, in addition to just working out. When you do so, your physique will change into what you want it to be. You have to imagine what you want to look like. You have to see what you will become. Then you start working toward that goal.

Jesus is coming back, but let's get something accomplished first! Let's get the whole world full of His glory. Let's have entrepreneurs who are multimillionaires and billionaires putting people to work, making people happy, and changing their world as they invest in the Kingdom of God. Is that a possibility? Jesus said, "...*If you can believe, all things are possible to him who believes*" (Mark 9:23). Let a picture of what you want to have or to happen grow in your spirit while you're praying. Use your *dianoia* now for your prayer life. Believe, and then receive.

Developing the creative side of your mind is thoroughly biblical. And I think it helps us to understand why the prayer warriors in the Bible could pray so long. Those men and women actually travailed in prayer. Travailing happens when the womb is full and birth is about to take place. It takes some work—labor, if you will. You engage your mind and you begin to see a picture of your dream's fulfillment within your imagination. And there's nothing like seeing your dream come true.

Did you ever go to a showroom and see a particular car and say something like, "Oh, someday I want one like that"? Then one day you actually get that very kind of automobile. If it works in the realm of cars, you can know for sure that it works in the realm of God's dreams for His people.

Yes, there are "piano people" who are reading this book. Some are "piano people" in the realm of education, and some find themselves in the realm of entertainment. Others are found in the realm of sports or some other sphere. Choose not to believe what others have said to you to limit you or discourage you; choose, rather, to see yourself becoming the best. God isn't satisfied with you being just good or even better; He is the most excellent, and He wants you at your best, as well. Now imagine that!

ENDNOTES

1. Kelly Mathew, *The Rhythm of Life* (New York, 2004), 35 – 37.

2. Maltz, Maxwell, *The New Psycho-Cybernetics* (New York, 2001), 61.

3. Neville, *Awakened Imagination* (Camarillo, CA., 1954), dedication.

CHAPTER 5

The Eyes of Your Heart, and Your Speech

God has given an imagination to everyone, and He expects us to use it. Paul refers to this in Ephesians 1, when he is praying for the believers. When we take a good look at this prayer, we realize that Paul knew that the Ephesian Christians weren't using their creative imaginations, so he prayed that they would be enlightened. He wanted them to start using the wonderful and powerful, God-given tool of their imaginations.

Paul prayed, "...*that you may know what is the hope of His calling, what are the riches of the glory of His inheritance in the saints, and what is the exceeding greatness of His power toward us who believe, according to the working of His mighty power*" (Eph. 1:18-19). People need hope today, and they need to know why they are here. In effect, Paul was praying that the Ephesians would see their purpose. What is your purpose?

Paul wanted the believers to know what the riches of the glory of the Lord's inheritance are in the saints. It is as if he is saying, "If you only knew how much God has given to you. If you only knew what you could use that you haven't yet accessed—*the riches of the glory of His inheritance in the saints.*"

THE POWER OF GOD

Then he takes it a step further, as he prays for the Christians. He asks God to help them know the exceeding greatness of His power toward us who believe. Sometimes we think we don't have any power at all, but Paul talks about *"the exceeding greatness of His power toward us who believe,"* and he goes on to say, *"...according to the working of His mighty power which he worked in Christ when He raised Him from the dead and seated him at the right hand in the heavenly places"* (Eph. 1:19-20).

Next he tells us where the Lord Jesus Christ is now. He is seated at the Father's right hand in the heavenly places— *"far above all principality and power and might and dominion, and every name that is named, not only in this age but also in that which is to come"* (Eph. 1:20-21).

In the second chapter of Ephesians the Great Apostle shows us how we have been made to sit together in the heavenly places with Christ Jesus. (See Ephesians 2:6.) With Him, we have been raised above all the beings in the universe, above all principalities, powers, might, dominion, and every name that is named. He is saying, "Look! You have power over the deepest, darkest devils in the universe. You have power over everything that is anti-God and anti-your success."

He is telling us that we have resurrection power available to us—that same power that raised Christ from the dead. God wants us to experience the exceeding greatness of His power toward us. Paul wrote, *"And He put all things under His feet, and gave Him to be head over all things to the church, which is His body, the fullness of Him who fills all in all"*

(Eph. 1:22-23). Jesus is the head over all things to the Church, which is His Body, the fullness of Him who fills all in all. We, as the Body of Christ, have not seen nor experienced all that this means—yet. We haven't partaken of the fullness of God, who fills all in all through His glorious Church. However, as we begin to see it, we will begin to participate in the fulfillment and answer to Paul's prayer, which God wants to see fulfilled in every Christian's life.

Remember, in the Bible *selah* means to pause and think. So take a selah faith break and pause for a moment and say, "OK, I realize something here; this doesn't happen overnight. It's just like a pregnancy. It takes time for the baby to develop fully. Similarly, it will take time to fully develop the goals you have set for your life. Never forget, though, that it will come to pass.

BE SPECIFIC AND DEFINITE

As you become "pregnant" with clear-cut goals for your life, get rid of vague prayers. Become specific with God. In this way God can release all the power in the universe to work in your behalf, and you will see answers to your prayers. So place your order with God. Be specific and definite.

When you go to the drive-through window of McDonald's or Burger King, I'm sure you are very specific about what you want. Be the same with God. He is asking, "What do you want?" What He's really asking is, "What have I put in your heart? Would you please begin speaking it?"

Use your imagination to see clearly what God has put in your heart. As you do so, you will experience feelings that go along with what you are seeing in your imagination. Begin to feel the picture that you see.

God Will Grant Your Desires

The Bible says, "...*The desire of the righteous will be granted*" (Prov. 10:24). I love this promise. Do you see how this Word from God has the power to revolutionize your prayer life? If you really believe its truth, I'm sure you have a smile on your face right now. I hope so, because I'm pointing you toward something that has actually been granted to you.

Here's a similar promise for you to consider: "*Delight yourself also in the Lord, and He shall give you the desires of your heart*" (Ps. 37:4). The Hebrew word for "heart," that is used here refers to the feelings of the heart. What are the feelings (desires) of your heart? The desires of your heart should bring forth feelings.

God is not saying that we should be devoid of emotions. Rather, He's saying, "I want you to receive something here, in the feeling center of your life." The Bible says, "*He gives power to the weak, and to those who have no might He increases strength. Even the youths shall faint and be weary, and the young men shall utterly fall, but those who wait on the Lord shall renew their strength; they shall mount up with wings like eagles, they shall run and not be weary, they shall walk and not faint*" (Isa. 40:29-31).

The Hebrew word that is translated as "wait" in this passage means "to expect and to bind together by twisting." This helps us to see what God wants from us. He wants us to imagine our prayers being answered. Waiting involves expectation, and, as you wait, you're engaged in your imagination, believing that God's answer will come. Waiting is an active involvement, not a passive idleness.

One of the ways in which Jesus is very different from all other religious figures is that He's not a religious figure at all. He is a living Friend with whom you can have fellowship. Buddhism teaches that Nirvana happens when you come to a place of total detachment, a place where you no longer experience desire.

Unlike Buddha, Jesus wants you to experience white-heated desire. He wants you to have desires. Did you know that the Bible has much to say about desire? One of the desires He desires for you is to be closely knit together with Him, so that you will spend a great deal of time with Him. This is like being all twisted up with Him, almost like a pretzel, and, when this is your experience, you just can't get out of your "entanglement" with the Lord.

COMMANDING FAITH

Your word is the material that the Holy Spirit uses to create things. You're waiting for something to happen, and God is waiting for you to do something. Too many of us have become beggars as Christians. We ask for money and many other things. We try to raise cash through telethons and other fund-raisers. We keep asking the people for money. In this sense, we've become beggars.

Moses begged God. He cried, "Oh, the Egyptians are coming. They're behind us, and the Red Sea is in front of us, and we're going to drown."

God said, "Shut up! You're using the wrong side of your brain, Moses, and you're using the wrong language! Tell the people to keep going forward. You'll make it. I'll part the Red Sea for you, if you'll just give the command."

Do you see how God gave Moses power through the words of his mouth? All he had to do was to command that the waters would part, and they did. Have we become wimps in the faith? Have we forgotten how to use commanding authority in our spiritual lives? Sometimes Jesus prayed all night long. Then He would go out on life's battlefields and enter the front lines. When He got to the front, He would issue commands. Remember how He commanded the sea?" He simply said, *"Peace. Be still"* (Mark 4:39). And the waters grew calm.

Likewise, He commanded the devil to behave—to shut up and get out. He commanded that people be healed. And His disciples learned to do the same thing. Peter said, *"Silver and gold I do not have, but what I do have I give you"* (Acts 3:6). Then he issued a firm command: *"In the name of Jesus Christ of Nazareth, rise up and walk"* (Acts 3:6).

Similarly, Peter gave a command to the corpse of Dorcas by saying, *"…Tabitha, arise…"* (Acts 9:40). Paul commanded the cripple at Lystra to *"Stand up straight on your feet!"* (Acts 14:10). In doing so, Paul was issuing a word of creation. This is a bold act on his part, and we're living in a time when great boldness of faith is required as we go forth into the world.

The Bible does not say that signs shall go ahead of you. It does say, however, that signs shall follow you. So get moving. Too many are waiting for a sign. "No," God says, "just get moving." Pray first, then start moving. Then the signs will follow. Don't be afraid to take bold action, so the signs will follow you. The Scriptures teach that our God-inspired desires should become our clear-cut goals. Then we are to start praying those goals with white-heated fervency.

James writes, "...*The effective, fervent prayer of a righteous man avails much*" (James 5:16). Make your prayers fervent, for it is the fervent prayer that will avail much. See it until you feel it. When you begin to feel it, you can really pray effectively.

This involves the use of your imagination. Then, as your visualization of your dream grows within you like a baby in a mother's womb, the time for its delivery and birth will come. This is the time for commanding faith to take over. You've seen it. You've spoken it in your prayers. And now the command comes forth.

Be smart and be wise about this. Do you remember the magicians in Egypt during the time of Moses? They performed some of the same miracles that Moses was doing. How did they do it? They used the creative sides of their minds and imaginations. The only problem was that their imaginations were linked to the dark side, but that doesn't mean they couldn't do anything supernatural. They did some of the same miracles that God enabled Moses and Aaron to do.

It isn't only Christians who can perform miracles. When I was a teenager, I thought that miracles happened only in the Christian realm. But I've learned better. When you go overseas, you can see miracles taking place among people of religions other than Christianity. Sometimes they even take place in higher-consciousness training seminars, as well; but these miracles are not linked to the Holy Spirit. They are not from the Spirit of Christ, and their practitioners don't claim that they are. They may claim, though, that their followers are gods, not only that they partake of deity, as our faith declares, but they declare that the people themselves are gods.

Jesus says, "Hold it, you're in me and I'm in you. Begin to let me live through you." Paul said, "*I have been crucified with Christ; it is no longer I who live, but Christ lives in me; and the life which I now live in the flesh I live by faith in the Son of God, who loved me and gave Himself for me*" (Gal. 2:20). That's the difference between miracles we experience as Christians and other kinds of miracles. Yes, there are some miracles that do take place in other religions, but they are not of the same caliber and do not come from the same source that the miracles of Christianity do.

THE CHALLENGING COUNTERFEIT

In the late '60s Raphael Gasson wrote an intriguing book entitled *The Challenging Counterfeit*. In this book Gasson shows the difference between supernatural manifestations in Christianity and those from other sources.

For example, he shared his experiences as a channeler or medium, one through whom spirits would speak to others. Gasson said that at that time he believed he was the channel for good spirits, which told him good things about people and shared the great things that would be happening to them.

He also told about a warlock who was putting evil incantations and curses on others. Gasson was challenged by the warlock, so the two men went under hypnosis, and, while they were in a hypnotic trance, the spirits within the warlock were chatting happily with the spirits that were using Gasson as their channel! Prior to this experience, Gasson had thought he was working with "the angels of light." However, when he awoke from the trance, he heard the tape that recorded this experiment with hypnosis. He was so stunned by what he heard that he voluntarily submitted to an exorcism.

The devil doesn't like to leave quickly, though, and that night Gasson said he awoke and the spirits took over his hands; this resulted in him clutching his own neck; his hands tried to choke him to death! He was only able to speak one word: "Jesus!" As he did so, the evil spirits left him.

The magicians in Egypt could do almost all the same miracles as the Lord's servants could, but when Moses threw down his rod, and it became a snake, and they threw down their rods, and they became snakes, Moses' snake ate up all the others! There is a big difference between Christian authority and occult powers. Jesus said, "*All authority has been given to me in heaven and on earth*" (Matt. 28:18). And He lives within you. That means that His power and authority are within you as well, and He wants you to use His power and authority wherever you are.

Psychologists talk about the realm of the subconscious mind. The Bible calls this realm "the hidden man of the heart." This is your spirit—your human spirit. Your human spirit can be developed to such an extent that it will be able to do great things, including miracles. But if your human spirit is aligned with a malevolent spirit, evil miracles and evil deeds may result.

My friend the late George McClain traveled the world. He was a famous Hollywood architect for a number of years, and he designed homes for many celebrities. He told me that it was a common experience, when he traveled to India with some of his successful celebrity buddies, to see some gurus flicking their thumbs and thereby producing light and fire from the tips of their thumbs. These Hindu gurus had learned occult secrets that enabled them to accomplish such remarkable feats.

Jesus, on the other hand, isn't interested in having us go around impressing people by having fire come out of our thumbs or doing anything like that. The miracles of Jesus are designed to help people, not to impress them with our own power.

Some people have joined their human spirits to unknown and evil spirits without realizing what has happened. This was the case with Raphael Gasson. This is very dangerous, indeed, because it can lead people down some very dark and foreboding alleyways of evil. Others seem very positive and enthusiastic, without any noticeable evil about them, but they stop at acknowledging Jesus as the Savior who took our sin on the Cross. All too often, they don't believe they have any sin for Him to take!

Some of the things these teachers say is good and their supernatural powers are often evident. This happens because they've learned how to tap into some of the laws of the universe that are unknown to most others. The sad thing is, though, that they can't humble themselves and submit their lives to the Lord. They can't lay their burdens down at the foot of the Cross. Neither can they cleanse you.

They can't offer or give you a fresh, new start either. They are very limited with regard to what they can do, but, as a believer, through envisioning and dreaming with your imagination, you can kick down all walls of limitation. God's Word says, "*Where there is no vision, the people perish*" (Prov 29:18 KJV). A number of Christian people are perishing because they have no vision. They don't seem to know how to envision. They don't use their imaginations because they've never learned how.

Become a Rock, not a Reed

Let me draw another mental blueprint for you. I want you to clear the canvas of your imagination and begin to draw a new picture in your own mind. First, however, let's look at an example from the Word of God. When Jesus looked at Simon, He said, Ah, Simon, you are like a pebble, but I'm going to make you a rock. (John 1:42 and Matt. 16:18).

Jesus was telling Simon that He was going to transform him from a little stone to a rock. Perhaps you see yourself as little, insecure, or a failure. If so, remember that Jesus wants to make you a rock. Never forget that you were created in God's image. The Word declares this truth to you. You were created in the image of God. You were redeemed by Christ. The Lord Jesus lives within you.

Therefore, as God's child, it is right for you to have a desire to enter the miraculous and to see miracles take place. Why? Because our God is a miracle-worker. We're His children, so we have that creative power and spiritual desire within us. We want to see miracles performed.

This means that the more you grow in Christ, the more responsible you will be to let miracles flow through you to an unbelieving world. I'm not talking about magician's tricks or fire coming out of your thumbs, but I'm referring to miracles of healing and deliverance, miracles of protection, miracles of salvation, and miracles of healing. We have a responsibility to supply these kinds of miracles to a lost and dying world.

There are plenty of magicians in the world today, and they are endeavoring to develop their subconscious minds in order to tap into certain powers; but God wants us to use our dreams and our visions for Him, so that we can perform wonderful miracles in His name and authority.

The Scriptures about these truths have not been dealt with adequately in the Body of Christ. There's a great need for us to activate our minds and imaginations in this area, so that we can have dominion in every realm of life and see God's miracles come to pass in our lives and the lives of others.

Through this law of faith you can give orders to your circumstances and situations and turn that which is ugly into something beautiful. You can bring healing to those who are broken, hurt, and suffering. That's the power that is available to you through your dianoia, or the creative side of your mind. God wants you to see, use, and experience the awesome power that is dwelling within you. Remember, we tap into that power by faith.

One of the world's leading neurosurgeons says that if a person understands that their speech center rules over the nerves of their bodies that it will change their lives. He also said that the speech center of every person rules over all the nerves of their bodies. What are you speaking forth? Are your words weak words or strong words? Do you say, "Well, I'm too old, and I'm too tired." If you make such statements, then it's true; you're too old and you're too tired! Or do you say, "I'm able to do this. I'm able to accomplish great things." What you say is what you get.

People are often amazed when they hear about a 97-year-old man who has run a marathon (26 miles). They are incredulous when they hear of a 90-year-old lady sky-diving. How do these older folk do these things? It's simply because they want to do them and believe they can do them. I'm sure they also give voice to their desire in front of others.

Recently I attended a Philadelphia 76'ers game as the guest of starter Sammy Dalenbert. After the game, one of the ballplayers made a comment during dinner about how he imagined his success before it ever came to be. He said that he imagined it in specific terms. Sammy also told me that he was having trouble making foul shots and worked overtime on the court to get better. His percentages still fell so he cut his proactive time and started imagining for 20 minutes a day making (swishing) all his foul shots. Immediately his percentages went way up. His coach asked him what court he was using for his extra practice. Sammy said, "I am practicing less and using my imagination, Coach." His coach laughed in unbelief. Like him, when we really believe the pictures we have seen in our imaginations, we can give life to them by speaking them forth!

CHANGE YOUR LANGUAGE

Before any of this can happen, however, you must change your language, for the words you speak give the Holy Spirit the proper material He needs to create the fulfillment of your dreams. In the process you do not have to beg; rather, you must take authority over the situation. How do we take spiritual authority over something?

The answer to this question is found in the Gospel of Mark. Jesus said, "...*Have faith in God*" (Mark 11:22). In the margin of some Bibles you will read, "Have the faith of

God." What does this mean, and how can we have the faith of God? Jesus answers this question clearly for us: *"For assuredly, I say to you, whoever says to this mountain, 'Be removed and be cast into the sea,' and does not doubt in his heart, but believes that those things he says will be done, he will have whatever he says. Therefore I say to you, whatever things you ask when you pray, believe that you receive them, and you will have them"* (Mark 11:23-24). This is the faith of God in action.

The Greek word that is translated as "ask" in this passage means "to command a thing that's due to you." So, you don't approach God like a beggar by asking, "Please, Father," or by saying, "Could I...?" You command those things that are due to you into existence with the spiritual power and authority that has been imparted to your through your faith in Christ.

In effect Jesus was saying to us, "Whatever things you command that are due you, believe that you receive them, and you will have them." Doesn't that change the sense of this verse? Jesus said, *"Ask, and it will be given to you..."* (Luke 11:9). This takes on a whole new meaning as a result of our new understanding of the meaning of the word "ask." This verse follows Jesus' teaching on the value of persistence.

When you approach the throne of grace, how do you ask? Do you beg or do you take authority? Do you approach God with confidence or do you come from a stance of weakness? Are you resolute or are you wishy-washy? Are you shaky or are you secure? Do you express your desires to God in confident expectation that He will grant your requests?

Take command. Command it as a thing that is due to you, and it shall be given to you. Seek and you will find.

Knock and it will be opened to you. It's not so much that you are commanding God; rather, you are taking command of the situations, expressing faith in Him, and expecting Him to come through for you. Prayer is not a last resort. It is an avenue of blessing that we must take each and every day of our lives.

Place the goal in front of you that God has given to you, and keep your eyes upon it. Let it become a white-heated desire in your heart. Begin to see it coming to pass. Envision it. Use your *dianoia*, your imagination, to bring it into existence. Gird up the loins of your mind, the reproductive part of your mind, and then begin to speak it. There will come a day when all the speaking you've done will become the command center for all the nerves in your body, and your desire will be birthed in your life. In other words, you will command the thing to happen, and it will have to obey you. You will speak to the mountain and it will surely move!

Paul writes, *"But what does it say? 'The word is near you, in your mouth and in your heart'"* (Rom. 10:8). What is this word that's in your mouth and heart? Paul says, *"that is, the word of faith which we preach"* (Rom. 10:8). He goes on, *"If you confess with your mouth the Lord Jesus and believe in your heart that God has raised Him from the dead, you will be saved. For with the heart one believes unto righteousness, and with the mouth confession is made unto salvation"* (Rom. 8:9-10).

Your word brings the Presence of Jesus into any given situation. Do you understand this? Your word invokes the Presence of Jesus. When we say, "Jesus saves," we're releasing the Jesus of salvation. Some churches only go that far; they only teach that your sins are forgiven, and there's a home for you in Heaven. In the same way that we can release the Jesus of salvation, however, we can release Jesus the Healer, Jesus the Deliverer, Jesus the Blesser, Jesus the Protector, and Jesus the Peacemaker with the words of our mouth. As we do so, people are set free.

We release what we speak because our words have power. So, as we give out the whole Jesus by speaking of His power, people are healed in body, mind, and spirit.

Like a thermostat, you're responsible for the climate and atmosphere where you are. You bring the Presence of Jesus into your immediate environment through your words. You have God on your tongue, and you can release Him into the lives of others as you speak His truth. You can release God in an elevator, at work, in an airplane, at the gym, in the classroom, or wherever you are.

This does not mean, however, that you should go into any given area swinging your arms and talking like a big shot. You need to walk humbly with your God. (See Micah 6:8.) You have to develop humility and the right approach in your life, and you have to be sensitive to the leading of the Holy Spirit.

You do this by talking to yourself first. Look in the mirror and start talking to yourself. Where is the Word? Where is the word of healing for you? Where is the word of salvation for you? Where is the word of protection, the word of peace, and the word of courage for you? Speak it. Line up a Scripture promise with that word, and speak it to yourself. As you do so, the nerves in your body will get the message.

It's not a one-time thing, however. It requires consistent, daily experience, practice, and exercise. Jesus is usually bound by your lips and your words. Why do I use the word "usually" in this context? Because there are times when God sovereignly intervenes; nonetheless, He wants us to be part of the process of healing. That's what evangelism is. That's what caring for people is all about. We become His hands, His feet, and we even become His mouth.

God uses you because you have faith, a growing and developing faith; He does not use you because you're perfect. He loves you and He has chosen to come down to your level in order to lift you up. He wasn't afraid to become a human being so you could become the righteousness of God through Him. You don't have to climb Mount Everest to reach Him because He's already come down to you! Now that is the God I can worship!

Who are the people God uses? Those who are growing in faith. He understands that people who are growing in faith make a lot of mistakes. Did you ever notice how all the heroes in Faith's Hall of Fame (see Hebrews 11) all had major flaws? They weren't perfect, but they believed God and He counted it unto them as righteousness and blessed them exceedingly. God will help us strengthen our strengths and eliminate our weaknesses as we continue in faith, but we must be certain to engage our faith. What a wonderful privilege He gives us to be co-workers with Him in the working of miracles. There's nothing more exciting than this. Now imagine that!

CHAPTER 6

Determined Imagination: Think *From* It, Not of It

Cognitive psychologists say that every thought carries an emotional charge with it. These charges push us toward or away from some emotion, perhaps anger or joy. Think about that for a moment. Every thought you think has an emotional charge within it.

Experts have done studies with people regarding the relationship between thoughts and emotions. They ask the people in the studies to say certain phrases five times, such as, "I'm glad I'm not a _____." Then they fill in the blank. They say this five times, and when they're finished, they feel much better. Then they change the experiment and have the participants say, "I wish I were a _____." The researchers discovered that this makes the people feel much worse.

Now, when you begin to thank God, you begin to see the power and the potential in your mind and your spoken word. No thought is completely neutral. Each thought will have an emotional impact on you in one way or another. One psychologist did years of research on thousands of subjects, in which he put a pager on his participants. The pager would go off at random intervals. When it would go off, the people who were wearing the pagers would have to write down what they were doing, where they were, and what they were thinking at that given time. During this same experiment, the pager would go off when the people were alone, and the researchers would say, "Now, what are you thinking?"

One psychologist reported, "Contrary to what we tend to assume, the normal state of the mind is chaos. When we are left alone with no demands on our attention, the basic disorder of the mind reveals itself. With nothing to do, it begins to follow random patterns, usually stopping to consider something that is painful or disturbing.

Entropy is the normal state of consciousness. To avoid this condition people are naturally eager to fill their minds with whatever information is readily available to them, as long as it keeps their attention from turning inward and dwelling on negative feelings. This explains why many people choose to spend such a huge proportion of their time watching television, despite the fact that they rarely enjoyed it. This is also why many people dislike solitude.

Solitary confinement is considered a very negative thing by prisoners. In fact, it is one of the most diabolical forms of punishment known to mankind. Solitude forces people to think, and most of the thoughts they think while in silence or in solitude are negative thoughts that become very disturbing to them.

IT'S ALL IN THE MIND

The average person experiences 185 billion mental images throughout their lives. Because of this, we have to learn to meditate in positive ways so we can renew our minds. Some Christians are not sure about meditation. They're so caught in their boxes that they say, "Well, I don't know about this meditation thing. You know, Buddhists meditate."

The Bible has a great deal to say about meditation. (See Joshua 1:8 and Psalm 1, for example.) The fact is, almost everybody is meditating on something almost constantly. What is your focus? What are you meditating on?

Let's imagine two people who have the same income—a very low income. One of these people is always complaining; he or she is negative, jealous, and always looking at other people with envy. The other person with the same income, on the other hand, has gratitude in his or her heart and anticipation for improvement. What is the difference between these two individuals? It's all in their minds.

You can have two people who make it to the very top of a company, and one will become very arrogant and prideful, always stepping on people, while the other is always trying to help other people. They both received the same thing, the same position, the same power. What's the difference between them? It's all in their minds! Their mental perspectives control their behaviors.

The God of this universe longs to touch us, to talk to us, to motivate us, to speak to our hearts, to guide us, and to lead us. One person may say, "I don't have any time for God, I just don't want to be involved with God." Somebody else may say, "O God, I can't get away from you, and I don't want to get away from you." So two people who have the same opportunity to fellowship with God make two different choices. What's the difference? It's all in the mind.

Paul says, "*...But we have the mind of Christ*" (1 Cor. 2:16). We have the mind of Christ! What a thought that is. Later, in Philippians, Paul writes, "*Let this mind be in you which was also in Christ Jesus*" (Phil. 2:5). This means that we should cast down every part of our imaginations (our minds) that does not line up with God's new-creation picture of us.

This will take hard work and great faith. When Abraham finally realized that God was able to do what He had promised He would do, the patriarch was able to say, "OK, you go ahead and take Isaac. I'll offer him up to you."

Abraham told the men who stayed at the bottom of the hill, "We're going up to worship and we will be back." Notice that he said, "We will be back." Abraham knew that God was able to resurrect Isaac if he died. How did he have such faith? Because it was real in his heart. He had incubated it. He had looked up at those stars and said, "Hey, that is my son, and all the offspring from my son. So, even if I take him up there on top of the mountain and sacrifice him, God will resurrect him. I know, because God has given His promise to me. He looked at those stars so many nights, dreamed the dream that God gave to him, and, thereby, the promise became real, active, and alive in his spirit.

Don't forget that you can control your world with your words and thoughts. Therefore, you always want to speak the right words and think the right thoughts. Everything you desire is already a possibility for you as long as you think it is. This is true, no matter what you dream for, think of, or desire. It might be a desired state of peace, success, promotion, prosperity, or anything else. Remember, it's already a possibility when you think *of* it.

Then, when you think *from* it, it will become over-whelmingly real to you. There's a big difference between thinking *of* something and thinking *from* something. How do you think *from* something? You do so when you begin to feel it and experience it. You think of a certain automobile's make and model, for example, and you say, "This is the car I want." You don't just picture it and think of it; you actually see yourself sitting behind the driver's wheel. You envision yourself driving it. You see its color, shape, style, upholstery, dashboard, and you feel the gear shift. Your eyes look out through the vehicle's tinted windows. You smell its new-car smell. This is thinking *from* the car, not just *of* it.

If you can see it, you can receive it. That's why Jesus talked in parables so often. He was giving people mental pictures; He was stimulating their imaginations with verbal images. You've got to picture it. But picture yourself *from* it. See it with your own eyes. When you see it from your own eyes, you begin to pick up some sensations. In fact, you will actually feel it.

When I've interviewed some major league baseball players on TV, many of them will say that before a game they can actually see themselves at the plate. They can feel their spikes digging into the soil. They experience all this in their imaginations. They visualize these things before they ever get into a ballgame. They can see the pitch coming, and they can feel the bat. They experience the adrenaline flow of their energy and they imagine the bat connecting with the ball. They can even watch the ball flying into the air, and they can see their follow-through after their swing. It is the same way in golf and other sports.

Jesus said, "*But seek first the kingdom of God and His righteousness, and all these things shall be added to you*" (Matt. 6:33). Always put God first, and see yourself winning people to the Lord. See them opening up to the solution you present to them, and soon you will attract people to you who are open to the Gospel of Jesus Christ.

DETERMINED IMAGINATION AND CREATIVE PRAYER

Determined imagination is the beginning of creative prayer. You begin to see yourself or someone else as being completely whole. Did you know that the future will become the present within the realm of your imagination? There, also, vision will come into being. You can see yourself winning an award. You can see your script being chosen for a Hollywood movie. You can picture the phone call you've been waiting for taking place. In fact, in your imagination, you're able to actually see yourself answering the phone.

This kind of determined imagination is the secret to prayer. It is the reason why Elijah could pray with authority and fervency. This is why James said, "*The effectual fervent prayer of a righteous man availeth much*" (James 5:16 KJV). You won't have fervency in your heart or in your prayers if all you see is defeat. When you see the victory, a smile spreads across your face. You feel it and you have the taste of victory in your mouth. That's what I mean about envisioning *from it*, instead of thinking *about it* in your imagination without emotion.

When this happens, the future becomes the present, and you actually get to see your desire fulfilled. Jesus said, "*Have faith in God*" (Mark 11:22). Then He went on to say, "*Assuredly, I say to you, whosoever says to this mountain, 'Be removed and be cast into the sea,' and does not doubt in his heart, but believes that those things he says will be done, he will have whatever he says"* (Mark 11:23).

Therefore, whatsoever things you desire with a command, those things that are due to you, because they're part of your purpose in life, will be done! Jesus promises it. And you can say to the devil, "You're not going to detour me anymore; you're not going to delay me; and you're not going to hold me up, because I've incubated and nurtured this desire in the "womb" of my spirit and now I'm giving birth to it. Therefore, you command, "Mountain be removed!"

You are going to receive what you say, what you envision, what you believe in your heart of hearts. You will see the fulfillment of your desire. Don't passively surrender to the evidence that is presented by your senses, for that will lead to depression. It might even cause you to say, "Well, I prayed but I don't see it."

I've noticed that many people will give up on prayer if what they prayed for does not materialize within a couple of days. They will say, "Well, I didn't see it happen so I'm going to give it up." They have failed to avail themselves of the dynamic power that is available to them. When the capacity of the Holy Spirit is joined to the human spirit, the law of faith is always activated. So join your spirit with the Holy Spirit and the Word of God. When you do this, you will begin to see what you desire actually taking place, and your feelings will flow with what you see. This will enable you to go from desire to satisfaction.

Don't ever stop at the desire level. Get excited about prayer. Persevere with your determined imagination. Bring it to the level of white-heated desire until you enter the place of satisfaction, the place where you actually receive what you are believing for. What a glorious moment that will be!

ESCAPE THROUGH YOUR IMAGINATION

Through your imagination you can escape from the limitations of your senses and the bondage of human reason. When the men built the tower of Babel, God came down to see the city and tower they had built. He said, *"Indeed the people are one and they all have one language, and this is what they begin to do; now nothing that they imagine to do will be withheld from them. Come, let Us go down and there confuse their language, that they may not understand one another's speech"* (Gen. 11:6-7).

Why did God want to confuse their language? It's because they were all speaking the same thing and seeing the same thing, and the imaginations of their hearts were evil. He knew that unless He did this, they would eventually imagine the whole earth into the wickedness and darkness of the evil one.

God is all-powerful, and nothing can stop you when you're in the Holy Spirit and the Word, and you are exercising the law of faith. In the Parable of the Prodigal Son the father says to his oldest son, *"Son, thou art ever with me, and all that I have is thine"* (Luke 15:31 KJV).

Jesus says much the same thing to us today. All that He has is ours—everything from the Gospels on through the epistles and the Book of Revelation. He has given us everything that is necessary for the fulfillment of our purpose in life. Paul writes, *"Blessed be the God and Father of our Lord*

Jesus Christ, who has blessed us with every spiritual blessing in the heavenly places in Christ" (Eph. 1:3). Look at all He has already given you—everything!

So, you see, life is much more controllable than what we may have thought. We have been brainwashed by the Darwinian model of random chance. This concept has run through our gene pool and it is nurtured throughout public schools. It is a philosophy that leads some to say, "Well, I'm just not made that way; the favor belongs to somebody else." Someone else might say, "I'm too short and fat," or "I'm too tall and thin."

The Lord, however, takes a different point of view. He says positive things about you. He believes in you, and He loves you with an everlasting love. There is a player in the NBA who doesn't have much talent in basketball. Can you believe there is actually an NBA player who doesn't have much talent? One basketball star said. "He is the worst player I've ever seen." But then he went on to say that this untalented player has so much heart that he always makes the cut and gets on the team. If you feel as if you're a nerd who is lacking talent in any given area, remember to apply the principles of this book, and you will become very successful in your chosen endeavors. You can become a winner instead of a loser—a victor instead of a victim.

Bob Dylan wasn't a great singer, but he could write outstanding music. As he put this strength to work, opportunities to sing opened up. He went from desire to satisfaction. It was not a random chance.

You make your own way, as well, because you have God on the inside. He's saying, "I'm with you in this. I'm equipping you and empowering you, but be sure to use your imagination."

You can travel much better along the mental highways of your inner world when you nurture great ideas on the inside. You will take action when you feel the power of those ideas. You have to feel it, though. Most people will not act until they *feel* the idea on the inside; it is then that they will move forward. Ideas awaken inner movement. When inner movement starts to take place in the highways of your mind, then outward movement will follow. But first it must be on the inside.

Therefore, it's so important for you to develop your inner man. God said to Joshua, *"Every place that the sole of your foot will tread upon I have given you, as I said to Moses"* (Josh. 1:3). Every place! What has God called you to do? See yourself doing it. See it in your imagination as you pray for it. Begin to speak that thing, line Scriptures up with it, and feel the joy of it fulfilled.

As you read these words, perhaps you're saying, "I'm feeling the baby move." I hope so. Once in a while you'll have some travail and some pains, but that's all right, just keep on pressing through the pains. The baby's coming. The dream is hatching. You are going to see in the manifested, visible world what you've already known and experienced in the invisible realm.

So start smiling when you pray. Why? You're seeing it as already accomplished, and that's something to smile about! Then you will move from the intensity of your desire (the inner craving) to completion, fulfillment, and satisfaction. Your prayer life will become very exciting, and you will be eager to get into prayer, because it will give you a glimpse of your future, and then your goosebumps will get goosebumps! Now imagine that!

CHAPTER 7

Your Focus Is Your Destiny

The Bible says *"Joseph remembered the* [his] *dreams"* (Gen. 42:9). God wants you to remember your dreams, because your dreams will keep you going. You see, God is very practical. He knows and wants you to understand that what you focus on will be what you develop in your life.

Your body responds to images. If you have a dream of a snake being in your bed, you may wake up and find (hopefully) that there's no snake in your bed, but your body will still be acting as if there was a snake in your bed! When you wake up after the nightmare, you find you're in a frenzy. You are in panic mode. You are perspiring, your pajamas are wet, you're shaking, and your heart is pounding out of your chest. Why is this so? Obviously, it's because you just dreamed there was a big, old snake in your bed.

The truth was, however, that there was no snake in your bed. Nonetheless, what your imagination had focused on had power over your body. There is great power in your imagination. Whatever you picture in your life will have power over your life.

What is a photograph? A photo is the transference of images by light. So if I focus on my wife in the congregation with a camera, what is going to happen when I push the button and the shutter opens? If I'm focusing on Ronda, but I am saying my son's name, "Isaac, Isaac, Isaac," will Isaac be in the picture? No, because I am focusing the camera on Ronda. Therefore, even though I am saying, "Isaac," it is what I am focusing on that will be produced on the film.

YOUR INTERNAL FOCUS

Some people think confession is the answer to everything. *This is not really true, for your focus is much more important than your confession. Why? Because you're focusing on something internally!* Eventually you will receive what your mental focus sees.

This may not always be what you are initially saying, however, because if you're saying it, but you're focusing on something else for most of the week, then you are going to be producing in your life what you have focused on.

Read Jesus' words in Matthew 6:22: *"The lamp of the body is the eyes; If therefore your eye is good, your whole body will be full of light."* In effect, Jesus is saying, "Have a single eye." A single eye of focus will bring help to you. God doesn't want you looking all over the place with regard to your purpose in life, because He has something specific for you. As you discover your purpose and begin to focus on it, your life will be transformed.

WHAT YOU SEE IS WHAT YOU GET

A few years ago, a group of weight lifting and martial arts entertainers came to our church and wanted to use me in a couple of their demonstrations. They stacked a large number of cinder blocks in front of me and said, "We want you to demonstrate the power of karate; you'll find you can learn it very quickly."

I replied, "Oh really?"

They said, "Yeah, you're going to jump up and come down as hard as you can with your elbow, and you're going to break those cinder blocks."

Incredulously, I said, "What?" I couldn't believe what they were asking me to do. You see, I've broken the arm I was supposed to use twice. I showed them my right arm and pointed out where the two breaks had taken place, and then I explained how my arm had been pinned together.

They responded, "That's OK, just don't look at the first block."

I said, "What do you mean? That's the block I'm going to hit!"

"No, no, no," they answered. "You have to look all the way down to the last block, because the energy in your body will be just enough to break the first block if the first block is your central focus. Instead, you've got to look all the way down, and see it through all the way to the end. When you do this, you're going to have the right amount of energy in your body, and, with a quick slam of your elbow, you will be able to go all the way!"

"Really?" I asked.

Do you know what happened? I was extremely surprised as I went up to the platform, took a deep breath, and, as they directed, put my focus on the last block, and brought my elbow down hard! I quickly discovered that they weren't trick blocks. They were the real thing, but they shattered all the way down to the last cinder block! No one was more amazed than I was!

I learned something from that experience. My instructor told me to keep my focus on the last block; he had assured me that the whole key to success in this endeavor was seeing through and following through. The important thing is to see the end result in advance.

The same thing is true in other aspects of life, for what you see is what will happen. What you see is what you will produce in your life. As was the case with my body in the demonstration I cited, your energy will go toward your focal point.

The truth is that you're either focusing on faith, or you're focusing on fear, doubt, unbelief, and skepticism. How do you save a friendship, or how do you save a marriage? How do you succeed at your job? How do you grow a church?

ASK THE RIGHT QUESTIONS

When you are confronted by a difficulty, an obstacle, or an unresolved issue, you must first ask yourself the right questions. All too often we ask the wrong questions. Many people begin by asking, "What's wrong?" I've done this, and I'm sure you've done it, as well. When I ask that negatively styled question, I quickly see five things to twenty things wrong! Someone might ask, "What's wrong with my marriage?" As you look for answers to this question, you may start with a few negatives, and then you pile many more on top of that one.

The right question to ask is: "How do I grow in the midst of this situation?" To be more specific one might ask, "How do I grow in this friendship?"; "How do I grow in this marriage?"; or "How does God use me to make this situation work?"

This more positive approach to asking the right kinds of questions will be a proactive, solution-finding way to deal with the issue or dilemma you face. Out of this more positive approach will come solutions and answers that aren't pulling everybody down into negative territory.

CHANGE YOUR FOCUS

Notice what Paul tells us to do in his letter to the Philippians: *"Finally, brethren, whatever things are true, whatever things are noble, whatever things are just, whatever things are pure, whatever things are lovely, whatever things are of good report, if there is any virtue, and if there is **anything** praiseworthy, **meditate** [use your imagination] on these things"* (Phil 4:8).

The apostle is saying, in effect, "If you're down to just one positive thing that you can think about a person, a job, or a church, the way you're going to help it is to remain focused on the one thing that's praiseworthy. This is cognitive restructuring and having your mind transformed.

You can't fix a problem by looking at the problem only. You fix it by visualizing something that works. Then, out of that positive mind-set, more creativity will come. It does not come out of what is wrong.

One of the best hitting instructors in baseball is Reggie Smith, who hit over 400 home runs as a switch hitter. He told me, "When I see a kid swinging, I find what they're doing right, not what they're doing wrong. And I increase what they're doing right to the point where they're so positive, that if there's a negative in their swing, they eventually will listen to me and then correct it."

Such a change comes out of a positive mind-set. It comes from the positive dimension. So if there's anything praiseworthy, meditate on that. This will lead you to a solution that will edify and bless everybody concerned. Your focus, whether it's negative or positive, will keep your energy flowing in certain directions. Are you going to let your focus give you positive energy or negative energy? Be careful what you focus on, for your focus makes all the difference in the world.

Take a lion trainer, for example. He goes into a ring with six ferocious lions and maybe even a tiger. He is armed with a pop gun and a little whip. Any one of these wild beasts could maul him at any point, or they all could "gang up" on him together. We watch breathlessly, as he turns his back on these creatures that seem to be ready to leap. Now, of course, if you encountered one of them in the wild, you would be totally terrorized, but this man stands in front of six or seven wild animals in a cage!

The animals snarl and growl and it seems they would like to have the trainer for lunch. Look at what happened to Roy of the "Sigmund and Roy Show" in Las Vegas. Roy was mauled badly by his "little baby tiger."

All trainers use a little stool when they are in a lions' cage. What is the purpose of the stool? It takes the focus of the lion off the man and puts it on to the stool. So, when the lion starts to roar, he will swipe at the stool, not at the man.

Each of us needs to use a "stool" in the same way a lion trainer does when we are threatened or attacked by the devil. You can be sure that he will try to send things your way in an effort to get you to focus on a certain lack, need, or problem. He loves to overwhelm you, because he doesn't want you to know how easy it is for you to get him under your feet.

Your success does not start when all your circumstances are wonderful and going well. It starts with your self talk. What kind of messages are you sending to your mind and heart? What are you telling yourself about the situation? Let your positive self talk be the stool you use to ward off the devil. Remember, he wants to defeat you in your thought life by showing you all the visible circumstances that are wrong or not working. Then he begins to roar like a lion, seeking whom he may devour. The more we hear his roar, the lower we may get unless we take our "stool of faith" and say, "I am a winner, satan! I am more than a conqueror through Christ!" Speak the Word of God to him, and he will flee from you.

Always remember that the devil never can defeat the Word. Put the "stool of faith" between him and you, and put your focus on the promises of God's Word. If you do so, satan and his demons won't be able to get to you.

As a follower of Christ, you have tremendous power available to you. Jesus said, *"Behold, I give unto you the authority to trample on serpents and scorpions, and over all the power of the enemy, and nothing shall by any means hurt you"* (Luke 10:19).

Thrust your Bible right in the devil's face. Remind him of the power you have as a believer, and don't let him affect your family, your checkbook, your language, your health, or anything else. Don't forget that he's after your imagination, as well. He knows that if he can get you thinking in a certain way, talking to yourself a certain way, and imagining the bad things that he wants to bring to pass in your life, he will have succeeded in getting you within his grip of unbelief and fear.

Take a good look at the truth, and you will find that you are facing a loser in the devil. In fact, he's already lost. Start building yourself up with the truth of God's Word. Resources follow vision and substance follows faith.

Walt Disney was the only man in the world who became a billionaire off a rat and a duck! He saw something that the rest of us aren't seeing, because he was a visionary. Your perspective is so important. When Saul saw Goliath, he cried, "Oh, he's too big to kill!"

When David saw Goliath, he said, "That fool's too big to miss!"

What are you seeing? What have you focused your gaze upon? Do you see only a problem, or do you see an opportunity? Is this problem going to paralyze you, or is it going to bring forth God's glory? Ezekiel said that the old bones he saw would rise again. (See Ezekiel 37.) He didn't just say that they were, old, dry, dusty, and dead. He saw them from a different perspective. God said to him, *"Son of man, can these bones live?"* (Ezek. 37:3).

The prophet answered, "*O Lord God, You know*" (Ezek. 37:3).

Then the Lord spoke: "*Prophesy to these bones, and say to them, 'O dry bones, hear the word of the Lord!'*" He went on to tell Ezekiel what to say, "*Thus says the Lord God to these bones: 'Surely I will cause breath to enter into you, and you shall live'*" (Ezek. 37:4,6).

The Lord then told Ezekiel to tell the people, who had lost their hope, these words: "*Thus says the Lord God: 'Behold, O My people, I will open your graves and cause you to come up from your graves, and bring you into the land of Israel'*" (Ezek. 37:12). This was a prophecy of vision and visualization, and it enabled Ezekiel and the people of Israel to focus on what God promised He would do.

In order to change your life, you must change your inner talking, the messages you send to yourself. Connect your inner speech to your imagination and let them both line up. Fill your imagination with fulfilled desire. On a negative level, many people do this all the time by connecting their imaginations to their sins and sinfulness or to worry, guilt, anger, or fear.

We must ever keep our goals and aims in front of us. What is your goal in life? Identify with it deep within your imagination. See it as if it has already been reached. The important thing is not where you are right now, nor what you once were, but the important thing is what you are aiming at—your goal. Keep focused on your God-given goals. This will always give you hope.

What you see is what you get. The more you see it, the more success you will have and the sooner it will come. Tell yourself, "This is what I'm going to produce" then keep seeing it as though it had already materialized. Let this become a central habit in your life.

Jesus told His followers that men ought *always* to pray and faint not (or lose heart). We ought always to pray. This, of course, doesn't mean that we must spend all of our time on our knees in conscious prayer. Instead, I believe it means that we can use our imaginations to connect with God all the time and to remain focused on the goals He's given to us. In other words, you can keep on dreaming and seeing the manifestation of those dreams within your spirit.

Any time you feel misunderstood, misused, neglected, suspicious, or afraid, you are wasting mental energy on negative thoughts, and this is a waste of your time. Don't spend your life away by living it that way. Instead, invest into your life. Whenever you are focused on positive goals, you are *investing* instead of *spending*.

You cannot afford to slip back into old, negative, thought patterns and expect to retain a positive command over your life. As soon as you give in to negative thoughts, satan has succeeded in defeating you. Paul tells us to flip it around and remember the praiseworthy things. Imagine those things, the things that are good, and find your way out of the problem.

START NEW MENTAL HABITS

To find a way out of any given dilemma, start a new habit in your mind. The negative customs and habit patterns we've learned through the years always tend to paralyze and immobilize us. Those habit patterns reflect your mental activity. The way you behave stems from your thought life.

Jesus said, "*Ask, and it will be given to you; seek, and you will find; knock, and it will be opened to you*" (Matt. 7:7). Every time I think about this verse I imagine someone, perhaps even myself, knocking on the door. But let's take it a step further. How about imagining the door opening as a result of our knocking on it? That's a different, more powerful picture. Then step into it by faith. See it actually happening. Walk through that door, don't just stand there knocking! See yourself seeking and finding. See yourself asking and receiving. Let this beautiful metaphor that Jesus gave to us become a living reality in your life.

GOD IS DOING A NEW THING

Something wonderful and dramatic is beginning to happen within the Church of Jesus Christ all over the world. This shift has already begun. We are beginning to see a fulfillment of this verse: "*Till we all come to the unity of the faith and to the knowledge of the Son of God, to a perfect man, to the measure of the stature of the fullness of Christ*" (Eph. 4:13). This is what God wants for us.

In order for this supernatural goal to become a way of life for us, we need to cultivate and develop a new attitude—one that we will always sustain and maintain. Jesus assures us that we can do anything that is God's will for our lives if we habitually conceive (Hebrew, *yester*) His will for our lives and act upon it. In this way we will give birth to it.

If we continually conceive the dreams and goals God gives to us within our imaginations, we will surely get excited about them, engage in fervent prayer about them, and visualize them coming to pass. Keep on speaking God's word of victory to yourself. Who you really are is not determined by what you say to me, but by what you say to the mirror and what you say to yourself while you are driving your car.

Let the things you say match up with the Word of God. As you do so, it will become a part of you and it will help you to see who you really are in God's eyes. Likewise, it will enable you to see and apprehend what is coming to you, because by faith you will know that it's already there for you.

Keep your focus on the things that are important and praiseworthy instead of on the things others say. Don't let anything or anyone distract you from the pursuit of your dream. As you focus on these things, you will find that a new, consistent mood will permeate your emotions and your thought life. Then you will begin to fuse with that mood, and you will be able to know and say that your ideas have power, because they have formed your focus and established your mood.

You will learn what Paul means when he says, *"Rejoice always, pray without ceasing, in everything give thanks; for this is the will of God in Christ Jesus for you"* (1 Thess. 5:16-18). In fact, you will be able to rejoice even in the midst of a bad situation. Won't that be wonderful? Won't that be a new freedom in your life?

Train yourself to see things differently, to see your dream being fulfilled. Don't give up, but keep on keeping on. By so doing your attitude will always be success-oriented, and you will see your goals being reached and coming to pass. You will learn to pray without ceasing, and when you reach that level of experience in prayer, keep it going. Don't forget it. Wear it like you would wear perfume or cologne. Let the fragrance of your prayer life and your positive imagination begin to affect all your responses, your reactions, and how you live every day.

This will happen because, by faith, you've seen something that is more real than the visible world. This happens because what you see internally will be produced in the visible world. If you want these changes for yourself, you must start with your inner self and be transformed in the spirit of your mind. These changes will attract all that God has promised to you, and His promises will begin to be fulfilled in your life. Your habitual moods reveal your state of mind and they show whether or not you're growing in faith. What are your habits?

Paul writes, "*And do not be conformed to this world, but be transformed by the renewing of your mind*" (Rom. 12:2). Notice how this verse points out that we are transformed by the renewing of our minds. When our minds are renewed, we are able to prove what the good and acceptable and perfect will of God actually is. Don't you want to prove that God's will is the best for your life?

When we know His will, we don't have to be always searching, always knocking, and always asking anymore. When our minds are transformed, we develop a habitual center of energy in our lives. Then we are able to train ourselves in all spiritual matters.

Therefore, it's vitally important for each of us to always look for a good report instead of listening to the negativity that swirls around us. We need to arouse the dream goals in our lives and let our emotions go in that direction, not toward negative concepts and things.

Have you ever noticed how easy it is to get your emotions involved when something is negative? Anger, depression, hurt, worry, and other feelings may overwhelm us at such times. Someone cuts in front of you on the highway and anger wells up. You have a dentist appointment, and fear begins to gnaw at you. Someone talks about you behind your back, and you feel hurt. A bill is due, and you begin to worry if there will be enough money to pay it.

Wouldn't it be wonderful if emotions followed the good things as easily and quickly as they follow the bad things we think about? When your mind is transformed, you will be able to experience a high level of positive emotions all the time—strong feelings that come from seeing what you desire and believing that it has already happened. You will see it as though it has already taken place. This changes your emotional perspective and it will create a positive mood and attitude that will attract others to you and attract the things you want toward you, as well.

Let an intensity of love and joy fill your heart. Walk away from criticism and dislikes. Be positive minded. Your whole life will change and you will be the catalyst that others need to bring about change in their lives.

God promises to give you beauty for ashes, and the oil of joy for mourning. (See Isaiah 61:3.) It's time to put on a new outfit and stop wearing sackcloth and ashes. Instead, wear the beauty of the Lord. Give your mourning to God, and let Him pour the oil of joy all over you. Keep saying the right things to yourself, and eventually what you say on the inside will be evident on the outside. Your life will change in noticeable ways. Your life will explode with a manifestation of the glory of God! In this way you will prove to the world that God's will is the most important thing. Now imagine that!

CHAPTER 8

The Master Key—You Have to Feel It to Produce It

Paul writes, "...*faith working by love*" (Gal. 5:6). He was saying that love-filled faith is the power that avails in a believer's life. Love feels. It is a strong, powerful emotion.

Feelings are central to the imagination. I must admit that I have missed this truth throughout most of my life. Now, though, as I go through the Word, I see it confirmed repeatedly. As I pointed out in an earlier chapter, when you think *from* something, from a fresh revelation of God's truth, everything changes. It enables you to see everything you need as being already yours.

Capture and hold the feeling that is associated with that truth for a moment. It's so exciting to know that the thing you desire won't be happening in the future, but it is happening to you now! Right now! How does it feel to know this? Train yourself to feel the way you would expect to feel if all the circumstances of your life were to line up in your favor.

Remember Jesus' words, which we've already pointed out. He said that all things are possible to you through faith.

Let the "high tide" of the feelings associated with this truth lift you above the "sandbar" of your five physical senses.

Don't get stuck on a "sandbar" in the "low tide." Boats that are stuck on sandbars usually have to wait for the high tide to come in before they can be dislodged. Live in the "high tide" of your godly emotions that stem from His will for you. Get in the flow of the Holy Spirit.

Remember that the Holy Spirit has His own language in which He delivers prophecies, speaks the Word of God, and gives dreams and visions that enable you to see what He wants for you and from you. This is the power of Pentecost.

THE POWER OF PRAISE

Praise is so powerful. Paul told us to focus on things that are praiseworthy—worthy of our praise.

So cast your cares upon Jesus and begin to praise Him for all that He is bringing to pass in your life. He loves you with an everlasting love, and that is a very praiseworthy realization indeed. Praise Him right now.

Always remember that you can praise God in your car, while you're taking a shower, while you are waiting in line, as you plant flowers, or while you are engaged in any other activity. As you praise Him, remember that nothing stands between you and the fulfillment of your God-given dreams but the supposed facts you create in your imagination.

Think about that for a moment: nothing but "facts" will prevent you from receiving what God wants to give to you. These "facts" are creations of your imagination. Everything we see and think about comes through our imaginations. If you change the images you see in your mind, you will change the facts. Praising God helps you to rise above those supposed facts and see everything from His point of view.

STIR YOUR IMAGINATION

The imagination is a wonderful gift, but Christians pay so little attention to it. Some are even afraid of it. Therefore, it is sleeping within most of us. You need to wake it up, and let it be stirred up within you. Don't bow before the "facts of life" and stand upon the foundation on which this whole world system is built.

This world revolves around ideas, concepts, philosophies, and ideals. All of these things begin in the imaginations of men and women, and they can be used for evil or for good. Unfortunately, the Church rarely uses this priceless gift.

Stir your imagination. Hold fast to God's ideals within your imagination. Take them with you everywhere you go. Never close the book on His will and His ways. Be persistent in imagining God's ideals as having been realized.

In order to prove to the whole world that God's will is supreme, you will need to walk by faith, not by sight. Many times faith is believing "the unbelievable," at least according to the standards of this world. That's what faith is all about—believing "the unbelievable."

In order to have this kind of faith you will need your spirit and your imagination. Let your spiritual imagination take you beyond the facts that are perceived by your five physical senses. Don't let your senses ridicule your dream and tell faith to depart. Train your faith to work by love, because love is such a powerful emotional force.

The "master key" to success in the spiritual life is the feeling and commitment that stem from love. Love enables you to develop self-discipline, and it leads you into a very successful and exciting prayer life.

As we have already pointed out, to pray successfully and effectively, you must have clearly defined goals and objectives in mind. You cannot ask for something unless you know specifically what it is. When you know what you want and express it to God in prayer, a wonderful feeling of love will envelop you because you will know that He has heard you and will be taking action in your behalf.

Prayer feels your fulfilled desire. Your state of mind will always capture your attention and take hold of your life. Think about that for a moment. If you have bitterness in your mind, for example, you will become critical and fearful, for that mind-set will have captured your attention and it will control your emotions.

Don't allow yourself to be infected with the poison that problems create. Don't focus on the past with all its losses, regrets, shame, and disappointment. Why even spend a moment of time or an ounce of energy on something that is over?

God, in His great love for us, tells us not to consider the former things, the things of our past. Get them out of your mind and out of your imagination. Why go around with regret? If you're regretful and you keep imagining what you regret, you're going to live in a regretful state of mind. Then you will keep attracting regretful events. Eventually, you'll find yourself going through regretful events over and over again!

NO DISTANCE IN PRAYER

Continue to pray fervently for what you desire. Think that God has already given the fulfillment of your desire to you. Oral Roberts wisely said, "There's no distance in prayer." In other words, when you engage in prayer, you move beyond your time-space constraints. Your prayer can affect somebody in Africa right now as you pray. There is no distance in prayer.

However, prayer depends upon your attitude of mind for its success. It doesn't require the attitude of its subject to be right, but the attitude of the one who is praying must be right. What is your attitude? You cannot give what you do not have and you only have what you believe.

Faith is the substance of things hoped for, and it becomes the evidence of things not seen. Keep on believing with a strong feeling of love and expectancy. In this way you will walk with confidence and you will wield a great influence in the lives of others. You will awaken their imaginations. When you pray for another, believe that what you are praying for has already come true in his or her life. Believe it about them. That kind of faith-filled praying always works. You can have whatever you say for them and for yourself, as well.

This happens when your imagination is activated to see, believe, and receive. Did you know that your beliefs have a sound? That's what is meant when someone asks, "What's your music?" They want to know what music is influencing your life. Does it have good vibrations or bad vibrations? What vibrations does your life send forth? Some send out vibrations that they know everything. Others send out more positive "vibes," such as, "I love you," "I want the best for your life," "I want you to know God," "I want you to find your life purpose," or "I want you to have your dreams fulfilled."

When Job prayed for his friends, even those who had ridiculed and abused him, his captivity was turned around. He could not have done so unless he had seen the fulfillment of his prayer for them within his own imagination. Job must have believed that they would receive and that God's Spirit was at work in them to bring the answers to pass. This is because Job knew how to trust God.

Throughout my life I've had to deal with many different mental arguments, strongholds that tried to deflect me from my walk with God. These develop within us from a variety of sources, such as the media, friendships, things at work, etc. We may watch a talk show on television, for example, and really get riled up about what is being said. We might say, "I know how I would have answered that guy." All too quickly we get drawn into the argument that is unfolding in front of us.

These "talking heads" engage in argument after argument, and they end up shouting at each other. Arguing causes us to get defensive and extremely competitive and we say, "I'm going to win this argument, or I'm going to show them what I really mean!" What do we do when this becomes our attitude? We picture the other person as either responding or asking another question, and then we plan our next response. This is what an argument always entails.

Then, the next time you see that person, you expect more conflict, because that's what you imagine. You begin to imagine the next argument, and you may even imagine yourself winning it. Obviously, this is the wrong focus. Instead, our focus should be on love for the other person, not winning some argument against him or her. This is love in action, and such love involves feelings, and it always sends forth positive "vibes."

SPIRITUAL BLINDNESS AND DEAFNESS

Centuries ago, Isaiah the prophet said, *"Hear, you deaf; and look, you blind, that you may see. Who is blind but My servant, or deaf as My messenger whom I send?..."* (Isa. 42:18-19). I believe this is a word to the Church today. Who is as blind as Christian people today? The eyes of their imaginations are closed. Scientists, artists, entertainers, and authors in the world use their imaginations most effectively, but where do we find active imaginations in the Church today?

Imaginations that see and hear receive answers to their prayers. You'll see this happen when you actually begin to believe that the person you're praying for is already the ideal man, woman, boy, or girl that you and God want him or her to be. In your God-given imagination see the person as being whole and complete in Christ.

Open the eyes of your spirit and pray for those who need healing or prosperity, then see them as healed and prosperous. In your imagination hear them saying, "I've never felt better in my life!" Hear them shout, "I've never been happier!" Rejoice with them as you hear them say, "I've never received so many blessings from God as I am receiving right now!"

Then picture yourself saying to them, "I'm so happy for you." See yourself crying tears of joy with them and saying, "I'm so happy for your life and how God is blessing you." See them and hear them as you want them to be, not as they are now. By doing this you will awaken that desired state in them and in yourself, as well.

You do this over and over again until it becomes reality. This is what Peter means by *"girding up the loins of your mind."* (See 1 Peter 1:13.)

Did you know that you can actually curse someone with the thoughts of your mind? The Bible says, *"Do not curse the king, even in your thought; do not curse the rich, even in your bedroom; for a bird of the air may carry your voice, and a bird in flight may tell the matter"* (Eccles. 10:20). Such a curse can fall on another because of your thoughts toward them; you don't even have to give voice to your thoughts.

We might tend to say things in our bedrooms that we would never say to somebody's face, but this could become a curse in their life. In other words, what you say behind closed doors has a life of its own and it puts forth vibes and music that go forth (are carried by the birds of the air). It can affect and infect the people you are talking about. Then, when you see them the next time, no matter if you're smiling or not, they will hear the music and sense the vibrations that you send forth. They may even know that you spoke against them. It is so much better to pray for them, bless them, and love them.

WHAT ARE YOUR DREAMS TELLING YOU?

Speaking of the bedroom, let's take a look at your dreams. The Bible deals with the subjects of sleep and dreams in many different ways. The study of dreams and their interpretation is very exciting and interesting.

Did you know that you can find out many things about the real you when you are sleeping? What are your dreams telling you? Before you go to sleep, activate your imagination by saying, "Lord, here's what I'm praying for, and I believe this is of you." Then, as you are falling asleep, begin to see it as accomplished. Do this with regard to your relationships, as well. See all the relationships of your life as being sound and flourishing. God will send "the music," even as you're sleeping, to the other people—the ones you are praying for.

The Bible says that God "...*gives His beloved sleep*" (Ps. 127:2). I believe a lot more happens before we go to sleep, while we are sleeping, and as soon as we awake than we may be aware of. Therefore, we do not want to close our eyes with negative thoughts swirling around in our minds, such as: "I'll get even with him tomorrow"; "I can't wait to tell her off"; "I wish she'd fall and break her ankle"; "I wish he was dead"; or any other negative curses. Those thoughts are seeds that are being planted in the fertile realm of your imagination, and they will influence your dreams.

CONFIDENT EXPECTATION

Confident expectation of a desired result is the most potent means of bringing it about. Anticipate it with confidence and great expectations. Many doctors say that one's belief in a cure is more powerful that the cure itself. A patient's belief in the treatment is extremely important.

The same thing is true regarding prayer and daily living. Such confidence can't be forced, however, but it does begin within the realm of your feelings. You desire something, then you see the desired result within your imagination, and then you begin to grow it in your center of hope. Your hope, as you hold on to it like the anchor of your soul, then turns into faith.

When true faith comes, you are able to say, "It doesn't matter that my senses are denying this thing, because I know God's Word has spoken it into being. So the circumstances and my feelings related to those circumstances don't matter right now." What really matters is your attitude in prayer. You begin to see it, and then you begin to pray it with feeling. We sing, "Let the weak say I am strong; let the poor say I am rich." This is a faith-building chorus, because it proclaims what you confidently expect God to do for you.

Some say, "That's denying reality." Not true. This response is actually saying that there's a bigger and better reality than my present circumstances and I can already see it in my spirit! God has given me everything I need; this is my inheritance in Him, so I'm just going to tap into His resources and release them into my life.

THE ART OF PRAYER

This happens as we begin to develop the art of prayer in our lives. Something that's artful doesn't wear you out, but striving does. Art is inspirational and creative; it imparts positive emotions.

Sometimes you might pray for five minutes and be totally exhausted. Why? In all likelihood it's because you don't really believe what you're praying. Your negative emotions take over, and you are defeated.

On the other hand, you can pray sometimes for half an hour, with an active imagination, and you feel refreshed. Where'd the time go? It went by so quickly because you were enjoying your prayer life. You were "having fun in prayer." That's what praying should be like—an artful, creative, powerful, and restorative activity.

Some American POW's in various wars have reported that their imaginations kept them alive while others died. Even as they were being tortured, they remained positive in their imaginations by simply closing their eyes and remembering basketball games with their kids, playing badminton or croquet, enjoying family cook-outs, and then imagining the future. They said they'd do this over and over again for hours, and they would fall asleep peacefully on the cement floor.

There's no doubt about it, the imagination is extremely powerful and you can use it to bring fulfillment, peace, and joy to your life. The Bible says, "*You will make your prayer to Him, He will hear you.... You will also declare a thing and it will be established for you; so light will shine on your ways*" (Job 22:27-28).

What are you declaring and decreeing? Decree what you want to see happen in your life and the lives of others. See your declaration being fulfilled in your imagination (your *dianoia*). By so doing your heart will believe it and experience the emotions associated with its fulfillment.

Speak it forth (that's what decreeing means), and your heart will believe what you say. Faith comes by hearing. If you don't declare it and believe it, you cannot receive it. Physical conditions can create psychological states, and the reverse is true, as well: Psychological perspectives can create physical conditions. Your mind has a strong effect on your body.

Jesus tells us to become like a child in matters of faith, wonder, trust, curiosity, innocence, and joy. He tells us to learn how His Kingdom operates and to discover the laws of His Kingdom. One of those laws states that if you believe, all things will be possible for you. Yes, all things are possible!

Your mind can cause you to be depressed or joyful. It's a choice you make. Let's say that your wife takes you to the ballet, "The Nutcracker Suite." You start dreading it before you even leave for the ballet. She loves it, but you hate it. You start saying to yourself, "I don't want to go the ballet. I'd rather see 'King Kong' than 'The Nutcracker Suite.'" Believe me, this will affect all your responses, even the way you treat your wife. If you take a different approach, however, the evening might turn out to be a blessing and a joyful experience. It's all a matter of attitude, and your attitudes come from your choices.

Awaken your feelings in prayer. To be effective, your prayers must be fervent, as James points out in James 5:16. The Greek word that is translated as "effective" or "effectual" in this verse means "powerful, active energy."

Where does such energy come from? It comes from deep within you. You provide it for yourself. The Holy Spirit activates it within your spirit as you choose it for yourself.

The Greek word that is translated as "fervent" in this verse means "to be hot, to boil with zeal."

You can't be hot and boiling with zeal without energy and emotion. You have to feel what you are praying for, and you choose to make yourself feel it. You can develop a steady state of mind in which the mood of expectant and artful prayer comes in, and you get excited about what's going to happen. You can always be effective and fervent in prayer.

The devil usually defeats us in prayer when we focus on our mistakes. Elijah was a man with a nature like our own. He dealt with the same passions we have, but that didn't stop him from praying. He prayed *earnestly* that it would not rain, and it did not rain on the land for three years and six months. Then he prayed again, and the heavens gave forth rain, allowing the earth to produce its fruit. Elijah prayed with powerful, active energy and fervency. He prayed earnestly, and you can pray the same way by utilizing the power of your imagination.

When you do so, you will be excited on the inside. You can experience this kind of prayer without ever uttering a word. It's better, of course, if you can get to a place where you can utter a word, but most of the time we are not in a place of silence. Therefore, we can pray silently within the sanctuary of our own spirits.

Someone might ask, "But the promise in James is for the righteous man." You are a righteous person if you are in Christ. He has forgiven every sin you've ever committed. Therefore, you can pray in full faith and expectancy, as Elijah did, and you will receive from God.

PRACTICE PRAYER

Prayer is an art form that requires practice, as all arts do. Jesus told us not to use not vain repetitions, but He did not say we shouldn't use repetitions. The key word here is "vain." Vanity involves self-centeredness and selfishness. Those things have nothing to do with faith. Whatever is not of faith is sin.

God will always reward your faith. The Bible says, *"But without faith it is impossible to please Him, for he who comes to God must believe that He is, and that He is a rewarder of those who diligently seek Him"* (Heb. 11:6).

Faith makes your prayer life come to life. It awakens the imagination of your spirit. This requires practice because you've got to develop the art of prayer in your life. Jesus said, *"But you, when you pray, go into your room, and when you have shut your door, pray to your Father who is in the secret place; and your Father who sees in secret will reward you openly"* (Matt. 6:6).

God will reward you *openly*. It will be obvious to you and others. In other words, it will be tangible and you will be able to see it. It's important to understand that you develop all this in the secret place, not out in the open. You don't go running around telling everybody about it. You develop it first on the inside. You say, "I thank you, Jesus, for showing this to me." Then you spend time alone with Him in your prayer closet.

As you go to bed at night, let your last thoughts center on a visualization of your desires being fulfilled. Experience the peace and joy that this brings to you.

THE MASTER KEY

A master key is one that can open every door in a building. There is such a key available to us in the realm of the spirit that will open the door to every blessing that God wants to shower upon us. That key is effectual, fervent prayer, the kind of prayer that is fueled by white-heated desire. Such praying will bring fulfillment to your desires, and you'll be able to say, "Thank you, Lord; it is done!"

From then on you'll be able to walk in confidence. This is a wonderful result of prayer. Isaiah said, "...*In quietness and confidence shall be your strength*" (Isa. 30:15). You develop this quietness and confidence in the secret place of earnest prayer.

The artful prayers you learn to pray in the secret place are not vain repetitions, fainting prayers, wishing prayers, or empty prayers. They are effectual, fervent, earnest, and confident prayers. If you truly love yourself and others, you're going to want the best for you and them. The best clearly is God's perfect will for you. As you learn to use the master key, you will begin to feel God's perfect will for yourself and them.

The energy field of love from the Holy Spirit will bring blessings to you and all those you pray for. So become like a child. Slip into your imagination and run your race to win. You will receive the Kingdom of God when you become like a child again and act upon your desires and your imagination. The manifestation will come. Believe those things that you pray and when you say them and believe them in your heart, as if you've already received them, then you shall have them. Now imagine that!

CHAPTER 9

The Reward for Strong
Desire and Perseverance

Do you want to stay where you are—spiritually, physically, emotionally, and financially—for the rest of your life? Why not? Aren't things OK? You live a fairly decent life. You have food in the refrigerator, gas in the car, and a bed to sleep in at night. You have a dog to walk and a cat that purrs, so why should you change anything?

Most people want to change something about their lives. Achieving the changes you want, however, requires a strong desire to change. It will also require a strong commitment, diligence, and perseverance. Life naturally seems to spiral downward instead of upward. People who are aging know this, and that includes all of us, because, you're older right now than you've ever been before! Yes, the natural spiral is downward, not upward.

I Am What This Book Says I Am

Even though the downward direction is the *natural* spiral, God has provided something better for us— the spiritual dimension through the New Covenant. We don't have to remain in the Old Covenant any longer. Let me give you an example. For years John Osteen would stand before his congregation and have everyone lift their Bibles and declare before the sermon, "I have what this Book says I have; I can do what this Book says I can do; I am what this Book says I am."

Sunday after Sunday the congregation repeated these truths. Little Joel Osteen grew up in that church. Every Sunday he declared with the congregation, "I am what this Book says I am." The natural mind might say, "Wait a minute! You're not there yet! You're far from it." The imagination, your spiritual mind, on the other hand, embraces this truth and runs with it. It declares, "I am what this Book says I am! I have what this Book says I have. I can do what this Book says I can do." When you reflect on those faith declarations, it puts a spring in your step and you truly get excited about life. As a result, Joel Osteen has become the pastor of one of the largest churches in the world and the author of a best-selling book.

A MASTER DREAMER

In Genesis 37:19 we read something significant about Joseph: *"Then they said to one another, 'Look, this dreamer is coming!'"* The phrase "this dreamer" means "the master of dreams" in the Hebrew language. There's no doubt about it, Joseph was a master dreamer, one who understood dreams and their purpose.

Joseph's brothers hated him, and one of the reasons why they hated him was that he truly was a master dreamer. Knowing this, they decided to sell him into slavery. They wanted to get him out of their lives. I think part of this was because, unlike his brothers, Joseph was one of the very few people who really believe that they will achieve their dreams.

Therefore, he was part of a persecuted minority. When you're a member of a select minority, you will make some other people very uncomfortable. Clearly, Joseph's brothers were uncomfortable with him and his ability to dream and interpret dreams.

We need master dreamers again. What you hope is what you dream. And that dream has to stem from great desire. We've already discussed the importance of the truths of Mark 11:23, which tell us that we can have mountain-moving faith as a result of the words that stem from our faith-filled imaginations. Jesus actually says that we can have what we desire. The Greek word Jesus uses here actually means "to lust." Lust, though it now has sexual connotations, simply means "strong desire."

This kind of lust involves *a mental effort that causes you to stretch yourself out toward the thing you have longed for.* That's what it means in the Greek. God wants to give you the desires of your heart. (See Psalm 37.) Your lust (strong desire) produces a vision within your imagination, and the Bible says that people will perish without a vision. No vision, no life. Without a vision people will die spiritually. Why? Without a vision there is no hope.

Without a vision your marriage, your family, your occupation, your work, and your church will suffer. A master dreamer always has a vision of positive change. Do you want to rule and reign in life? You can you know, especially if your heart's desire is for change.

Every father has dreams for his children, and your heavenly Father has dreams for you, as well. He wants you to tap into and embrace His spiritual laws so that His dreams for you will be fulfilled. All too often we focus on the problems of life. We see the problem, say the problem, fear the problem, pray the problem, and then we go around wondering why we have the problem.

Launch Out Into the Deep

Your focal point will either release fear or faith into your heart and life. If you've been releasing fear in your heart throughout most of your life, aren't you ready for change? Don't be afraid to branch out and launch out into the deep. Don't be afraid of failure. God loves it when His kids walk out on the water because He knows that when we go forth into unknown realms, our hope will grow into substance and our faith will grow into reality.

So become a part of the "faith minority." Get excited about it. Remember, Jesus is always with you, and He will pick you up if you fall. The world doesn't treat its failures well, but Jesus brings new life, new opportunities, and restoration to His children. When we fall as we endeavor to walk by faith, Jesus picks us up and says, "I'll walk you back to the boat!"

The Bible tells us that hope delayed or deferred makes the heart sick. (See Proverbs 13:12.) There are times when we must wait for what we want, however, because God wants to develop patience in our lives. The word "patience" in the original Greek means "cheerful endurance." So cheerfully endure as you await the fulfillment of your dreams.

Wait With Perseverance

Paul writes, "*For we were saved in this hope, but hope that is seen is not hope; for why does one still hope for what he sees?*"

(Rom. 8:24). We persevere through hope and joy. We expect God to come through for us. We endure in the face of some of the troubling circumstances of life, and we are able to keep on keeping on with a smile, because of the joy that God has set before us. In fact, we can tap into some of the future joy in the here-and-now of our lives.

It is this kind of perseverance and endurance that enables us to say, "I am already what I want to become. It has already happened." You can say, "I've already become what I hope to be!" Then you will start acting as if you believe it.

The Holy Spirit will help you. Paul writes, *"Likewise the Spirit also helps in our weaknesses..."* (Rom. 8:26). A weakness is an infirmity, and this connotes an inability to produce results. The Holy Spirit has been sent to your aid; He will enable you to produce results.

What is your weakness? What is your infirmity? God understands what you need, and your inability to produce results in that given area of your life will be transformed into ability and strength through the power of the Holy Spirit, who is your divine Helper.

We may sometimes think that the Holy Spirit helps us only if we're bending our knee in prayer or doing some good deed for another person. Certainly, He does help you in your prayer life and He empowers you to good deeds, but He also is the Helper who will help you produce what you've been unable to produce in your life; He will help you fulfill your destiny.

So invite the Holy Spirit into your life and become a partner with Him. Learn to speak His language through dreams, visions, and the Word of God. Let Him activate the power of your imagination. Speak His language so you can have true communion and fellowship with Him. In this way your imagination will be activated and the Holy Spirit will help you create reality and substance from your faith.

God's looking for people who will rise up in the midst of darkness and say, "Bless God! I can't count on my sense experience, and I'm not going to be ruled by this outward storm I'm going through. I can't help it if I can't see very far right now, but I'm going to stand firm in the midst of this darkness and ride out the storm in faith. God's going to see me through, and He is bringing His light to me in the midst of the darkness."

As faith overcomes fear, you will be able to praise God, and declare, "I'm going to see the best of this. I'll know no man after the flesh. I'm going to know these brothers and sisters after the spirit. I'm going to look for the best in them, not the worst. I'm going to rise above the circumstances. I'm a winner, not a loser!"

SPIRITUAL BATTLES REQUIRE SPIRITUAL POWER

When we learn to stop wrestling with one another and realize where the battle really is (in the spiritual realm), we will learn how to be victorious. Too many of us experience defeat as a result of our experiences with other people. We too easily forget the words of Paul: "*For we do not wrestle against flesh and blood, but against principalities, against powers, against the rulers of the darkness of this age, against spiritual hosts of wickedness in the heavenly places*" (Eph. 6:12).

The real battlefield is in the spiritual realm. So fight the battles with the spiritual weapons God has given to you—the Word of God, the power of the Holy Spirit, the blood of Jesus Christ, the word of your testimony, and the power of your faith-filled imagination. The Holy Spirit is saying, "If you'll just start imagining who you'll really be, and that you're already there, even before you see it, you're going to have the feeling of having accomplished it." And there's nothing better than the feeling that comes from accomplishing something.

It is then that you will be able to say, "I've done it!" It's not all about ability. It's more about you joining with the Holy Spirit, who promises to help you in all your infirmities. The world and many people within the Body of Christ won't understand that, but you do. While the world says, "Give us the best-looking the brightest ones, and the most talented among you to fill the top jobs in industry," the Christian says, "The weak will confound the wise." (See 1 Corinthians 1:27.)

God loves to take the weak things of the world and turn them into giants. He says, "I am going to make you *numero uno*. You will be strong, not weak. You will be the head and not the tail. You will be above and not beneath."

I remember how I idolized T.L. Osborn when I was a teenager. In my opinion, he was the greatest missionary of the 20th century. I knew he had spoken to hundreds of thousands, if not millions, of people around the world, and God had blessed his ministry with phenomenal miracles. So, when I heard he was coming to our area, I cranked up my old '55 Chevy, got my beautiful wife, Ronda, and headed out to hear the man of God speak. I was really excited to know that I was going to see him and hear him.

I wondered if my car would make it to the meeting, though, because it needed a new quart of oil added to the engine very 40 miles or so, and the white smoke kept pouring from the exhaust. When we arrived at the meeting, I wondered, "Where is the man of God?" I had never actually seen him in person, though I had seen his picture, but I didn't really know what he looked like.

In my mind's eye I had pictured a giant of a man, a magnificent superman. In a few moments a little guy came walking out onto the platform. I thought this must be his associate, someone who would be introducing T.L. Osborn. No, the short, little man was T.L. himself!

He took a small Bible out of his pocket and began speaking, but I could hardly hear what he was saying. He wasn't loud. He spoke softly and gently, but the Spirit of God moved mightily among us, and I'll never forget that wonderful night.

When you know who you are in God, you can be whatever He wants you to be. I learned later that Osborn could preach with a fiery and dramatic power, but that night the Holy Spirit moved more peacefully. T.L. Osborn knew that his job was to please God, not people, and I know he pleased God with his obedience to Him that evening.

Appearances can be so deceiving. Perhaps Samson, for example, looked like Woody Allen. We don't know what he looked like, of course, but how he looked is not the important thing. It's not the outward appearance that counts, but the inward power. It's the Spirit of God within a person that counts.

It's not you, but the Spirit of God within you that counts. Do you realize that you have access to God's wonderful, big Holy Spirit? The world doesn't have access to Him, but you do. You don't have to be the best-looking, the most talented, the brightest, the best-educated, or the greatest in any given area, because you have the Greater One within you. All you have to do is keep on lusting after God and His will for your life. He promises that He will join together with you and become your partner. He promises to help you in your infirmities.

All you need is a strong, craving desire for Him and His help. That desire is the "high tide" that will lift you easily above the sandbars of life, the places where most people get stuck. Embrace the mood which comes when you are able to envision that desire being fulfilled.

Nothing stands between you and the fulfillment of God's dream for your life except the supposed "facts" that are a creation of your imagination. Put those "facts" aside, then change your focus. Make a mental shift and use your God-given mind and imagination in the way God wants you to do. Stir your imagination to see the fulfillment of all your dreams, and you will begin to see dramatic changes, and the "facts" will change, as well. Remember that feeling and sensation always precede manifestation. Change these things, and you will change your destiny.

A CHILD-LIKE IMAGINATION

How many times do you hear the words "make believe" from kids? They will say to one another, "Let's make believe." They want to enter the world of their imaginations.

In so doing they pretend that they are Wyatt Earp and Doc Holliday, who are out to defeat the bad guys, or a little girl might pretend that she is Queen Esther. Whatever the case, the child actually "becomes" that person in his or her imagination.

When I was a child, I sometimes wore a cowboy hat and played with a toy gun. I remember that such play was always very real to me, because through the windows of my imagination I was actually able to enter the Wild West and become a hero.

We can do similar things with our imaginations as adults. In fact, we can actually change our environment through imaginative and creative power. We accomplish these things through cognitive restructuring, praying, "faithing it out," and utilizing the power of our imaginations. You might put some pictures that line up with your desires on your refrigerator or around the house, for example. This will help you to focus on what you are heading toward. See your desires materializing in front of you. See them as if they have already been achieved.

RENEW YOUR IMAGINATION

Progress in the spiritual life springs from your renewed imagination. It springs forth from your lust and your strong desire. If you really crave change for the good, then God will take you to another level. What you truly must feel, though, is that with your God-given imagination, all things are possible for you.

In every moment of your life, either consciously or unconsciously, you are assuming a feeling. As you are reading these words, you are experiencing certain feelings. You may not be conscious of all your feelings at any given time, but nonetheless they're there.

God wants you to learn how to control your feelings and your imagination (*dianoia*); it is a tool He has given for you to use to accomplish His purposes in and through your life. James writes, *"But be doers of the word, and not hearers only..."* (James 1:22). What does this mean? We may hear a word from God and think, "OK, I've got it." Unless we follow up on that word and actually incorporate it into our lives, however, it will not take effect. We must become doers of the word.

As we become doers of the word, we will experience fresh and wonderful feelings every day of our lives, and these feelings will stem from the realization that are desires have been fulfilled and are being fulfilled. Such feelings always come when you know you are actively participating in God's plan.

Nothing is ever accomplished through passivity. When one is a doer, however, mighty changes take place. You begin to attract all that you believe you are and all that you believe you have. You must believe you are the person you want to be in God. You're not a forgetful hearer; you are a doer of the word.

As such, you keep the feeling of fervent, hot desire stoked every day of your life. You learn to daydream with purpose. You pray effectual, fervent prayers and you realize that you are a member of a royal priesthood. You know that you already have the victory!

As a father, I want my son to stand up and walk in confidence that his God is the one, true God and that He is the one who shall make him more than a conqueror. As Ronda and I agree with him every day and in every way, he will learn to daydream with purpose. This is what the Father wants for you, as well. Start to see your dream as being fulfilled already. Don't see yourself as just trying to get there, for you are there already!

At this point someone might say, "I know God wants me there, but it's so hard to see. I see the failure and I see the pitfalls." For a while this kind of positive thinking and imagining will seem unnatural to you. You've been trained to think from the left side of your brain according to rational standards and your five physical senses. But the time will come when it will be very natural to see the things you want for your life as though you've already achieved them. When this happens, you will know the manifestations are close at hand.

Like any natural law, this spiritual law is inviolable. It always works. Like electricity, it can work for anyone who knows how to use it. God is saying, "I want my people to turn the switch on. I want them to change the world through the power I've put within them."

But you won't get there unless you learn to use your imagination for God. You need to worship Him in spirit and truth. Jesus said, "*You shall love the Lord your God with all your heart, with all your soul, and with all your mind*" (Matt. 22:37). That includes your imagination. You can worship God with your imagination.

When we begin to worship God in this way and get in tune with His perfect will, we will see what our destiny on this earth truly is and we will feel that we, as a body, have already accomplished His purposes through His power and might. We don't have to wait for the Rapture for this to happen. When Jesus comes back, the Bride of Christ is going to be beautiful on the earth; in the midst of the darkness there will be a people of light. We will be a people of glory—Zion, the joy of the whole earth. We will fill the earth with the glory of God, as the waters cover the sea.

On our journey to that wonderful climax of human history we should persevere. We need to be like Jacob who wrestled with the angel and said, "I will not let you go unless you bless me." We need to be like the Shunammite woman who knew Elisha had God's power. We need to be like the importunate widow who kept going back to the unrighteous judge until he did what she requested.

God is the righteous Judge. He moves in response to our perseverance. So pray without ceasing. Pray with strong desire and perseverance. This will bring you pleasure in prayer. Why? Because in this way you will see your desires as being fulfilled, and what could be more pleasurable than that? Declare it by faith: "I already am what this Book says I am! I already have what this Book says I have! I can already do what this Book says I can do!" Now imagine that!

CHAPTER 10

The Real Reality—Truth Is Stranger Than Fiction

M any times the truth really is stranger than fiction. Many of the things we see in the world were first developed in someone's mind and imagination. It was said, for example, that Michelangelo could see the figure he wanted to carve embedded in the block of marble before he began to sculpt it. He felt it was his job to release the figure that was entrapped within the marble.

In 1898 a struggling author, Morgan Robertson, wrote a novel about a fabulous ocean liner (the Titan), a vessel that was larger than any ocean liner that had ever been built. As his story developed, he said that the ocean liner struck an iceberg late one night in April and all its passengers were killed. He entitled his book, *Futility*. The people on board his imaginary ship were very wealthy, but their money was not able to help them get out of this horrible situation. He said that their wealth was in the neighborhood of $250 million!

Fourteen years later, Whitestar Lines built a steamer that was very much like the one described in Robertson's novel. It was the Titanic. It weighed 66,000 tons. Robertson's fictional ship had weighed 70 thousand tons. The real ship was 882.5 feet long, and the fictional ship was 800 feet long.

Both could carry approximately 3,000 people and both had an inadequate number of lifeboats for the number of people on board.

Interestingly, both had been labeled as unsinkable. However, on April 19, 1912, the Titanic left Southampton on her maiden voyage to New York. Her passengers were rich and they were complacent. Along the way she struck an iceberg and went down on that bitterly cold April night!

Could today's fiction be tomorrow's fact? In the world of sense we see what we have to see; but in the world of imagination we begin to see what we want to see. Then, when we see it, we begin to create it. As a result we create something that the senses can now behold. With the power of our imaginations we bring it into existence.

True Reality Begins in Your Mind

What is real? True reality starts in your mind.

When we pray things as they ought to be, we enter into an experience that is both fun and meaningful. There is no reason for any Christian to live in uncertainty. Jesus came to give us an abundant life. (See John 10:10.) We can make life abundant for ourselves and other people when we learn to pray as the prayer warriors in the Bible did. They were able to pray with confidence because they saw their prayers and dreams as being fulfilled.

One survey that was conducted among church people in a certain country showed that 95 percent of the church attendees were able to tell the surveyors why a dream won't work. They told the researchers that they didn't believe that their own dreams would ever be realized. Only 5 percent of these Christians believed that what they dreamed would ever be achieved.

Do you see how satan is a master at programming the human imagination? People worry, and they begin to picture their worries coming to pass. They picture the fulfillment of their worries! Likewise, they picture their doubts as coming true. That's how we've been trained to think. It's also how we've been programmed to pray.

Imagine what would happen if we could use the same energy that we use for worrying to picture our dreams coming true and our prayers being answered. Many prayer meetings in churches today are boring and depressing, and I believe that's why so few people attend such meetings.

You won't find boring prayers or prayer meetings in the New Testament. None of Jesus' prayers were boring and depressing because He was so sure of the things He prayed about. He had seen what the Father was doing, so He clearly knew how to pray. How was He able to see these things? Through the power of His imagination, which was connected to His spirit. This enabled Him to pray a quick prayer with full confidence that it would be answered. He prayed, "Be healed," and the person was healed. He prayed, "Rise up," and the person arose. He prayed, "Peace, be still," and the tempest ceased.

This same Jesus said, *"Most assuredly, I say to you, he who believes in Me, the works that I do he will do also; and greater works than these he will do, because I go to My Father"* (John 14:12). Greater works than the ones He did? Yes!

The great entrepreneur Andrew Carnegie was raised in the Midwest. His father was a poor farmer who told him, "You'll be a poor farmer the rest of your life."

Andrew refused to listen to the words of his father's prophecy. Instead, he developed a different picture in his imagination. At age 16 he borrowed his first $100. By the end of his life over a hundred years ago, Andrew Carnegie had given over $2 billion to charity.

How did he get to the point where he was able to be such a philanthropist? He said, "No. I'm not going to be a poor farmer. I see something else for my life!" He must have known that reality does not consist only of what one sees on a material and physical level.

Everything that is tangible is held together by molecules. As mentioned in a previous chapter, some scientists now talk about the string theory. They believe that sound holds the molecules together. I like that concept, because it seems very biblical. John wrote, *"In the beginning was the Word, and the Word was with God, and the Word was God"* (John 1:1). Yes, the Word (sound) holds everything together.

The images that are stimulated by your imagination are the realities of your life. And, in a sense, they release a sound. They will eventually manifest in your life. Though what you see may be only a shadow at times, always remember that it will make room for something else even if it disappears.

We've got to train the creative side of our minds to picture what God wants. He wants you to be victorious and to enjoy your life. Even when Paul was in prison, he was able to rise above the rats nibbling on his toes by not thinking about the rats, but thinking only on things that were good. The power of his imagination enabled him to rejoice even in a dirty and damp dungeon!

OUT OF THE ABUNDANCE OF YOUR HEART

We believe that if we just say the right thing, confess the right words around the right religious people, and say what we know they want to hear, that's all we need to do. But did you know that what you see counts for more than what you say? The Bible says that you will speak out of the abundance of your heart.

What abounds within your heart? That's what you will end up saying. What you dwell upon will come forth. Many Christians don't know what they really want in their lives. Often, Jesus asked people to tell Him specifically what they wanted Him to do for them. He did this for a reason—so that they would identify it, speak it, and see it!

Keep the ideal in your heart as you walk in the real world. Don't pretend that reality is not real, but do understand that there's a more real reality beyond the reality you see—another reality, a better reality. The Word of God reveals what that better reality is, and you enter that reality with your God-given imagination.

Let the Word of God produce the proper images in your spirit—the images that God wants you to hold on to. To young Timothy, Paul said, *"Let no one despise your youth..."* (1 Tim. 4:12). Then the apostle went on to say, *"Do not neglect the gift that is in you, which was given to you by prophecy with the laying on of the hands of the eldership. Meditate on these things; give yourself entirely to them, that your progress may be evident to all"* (1 Tim. 4:14-15).

What are the things that Paul wanted Timothy to meditate upon? It was the positive, prophetic word that was given over his life. He took that prophetic word and stirred it up within himself. This enabled him to keep on envisioning it and seeing it in his imagination as already having been fulfilled.

Part of that prophetic word is found in Second Timothy 1:7: *"For God has not given us a spirit of fear, but of power and of love and of a sound mind."* A sound mind is one that knows what to meditate on and how to control one's life and destiny. A sound mind uses the imagination to bring forth what God wants. A sound mind focuses on the good things and gives no time or thought to other things. A sound mind thinks on things that will make other people happy. It thinks about ways to help people.

Scientists tell us about a little creature known as the planaria. The planaria is a tiny flatworm. It's interesting to know that if you cut the planaria in half, it will grow another head from its back side. Amazingly, it is able to reproduce itself when it is split in half!

What can we learn from this little worm? God has put within us the power to heal and the power to live a rich and full life. Some people have been put in situations that were seemingly impossible to escape from and they thought that there was no way they could ever get out of those situations! They needed the power of the lowly planaria to overcome their situations.

At Shore Christian Center Church we had a worshiper who had spent some time in the penitentiary because he had killed a man. He became a Christian while he was in jail. Now he's out of jail, and he's demonstrating God's power and witnessing for Christ. That man was shot in the head, and the doctor said there was no way he should be alive with that bullet in his brain. They never removed the bullet because of its sensitive location.

It's amazing to see what the will to live and an attitude of "I'm not done yet" can accomplish. Yes, truth is stranger than fiction. Do you understand the potential that lies within you? Even if the worst happens and you lose your head (as all of us may frequently do), you can regrow it!

The next time you make a mistake tell your wife, "I'll regrow it, honey. I'll change." Don't see people as they are; see them as they ought to be. Let that picture develop within your imagination. If you are a teacher, see your students as they ought to be. As a coach, see your players as they ought to be. As a pastor, see your people as they ought to be. Your imagination has the power to change them.

When I coached baseball, our team, the Jersey Angels, won tournaments that we never should have won. It seemed as if we were among giants sometimes. We played against teams that millionaires in other states had put together, and we beat them! Our guys were little, but every day I taught them that nothing's impossible.

They noticed and thought about the sign that was posted in left field: Miracles Still Happen! And they lived out what they saw. I used to call them "the cardiac team," because they would frequently be losing until the ninth inning came along, and then they would outscore the other team. It's because they never gave up.

Like the Jersey Angels, you can be a winner too, and you can help others become winners, as well. All it takes is seeing yourself and other people as they ought to be instead of as they are. In this way you help them to transform themselves. Focus on the potential that dwells within every person, including yourself.

Moses stammered his way to freedom for the Hebrew people. God saw the potential that was within him, and Moses began to apprehend it, as well.

In the 1960s, a Yale homiletics professor said that the greatest orator in America was Oral Roberts. Roberts was a young preacher who spoke with an Oklahoma accent. If you are ever able to get any of his old tapes, listen to him. You will notice that his diction, his inflections, and his grammar were amazing. With eloquence and without notes, he'd speak about God and the wonderful Holy Spirit for an hour and a half, and people would sit there with rapt attention.

Then he would pray for people for hours. There was nobody who could speak like Oral Roberts, but did you know that he stammered and stuttered in high school? I noticed one time when he got particularly excited in one of his meetings that he began to stutter again while he was preaching. He dealt with it by simply saying, "satan, I rebuke you in Jesus' name!" He pulled right out of it, because he saw the God within him as being far greater than the one who was trying to stop him.

You may be stammering now or you may be stuttering. People may look at you and say that nothing good can come out of you, but God sees you in a different way. He sees you as a world-changer and a world-shaker. The world hasn't seen anything yet. The real reality is on its way. Now imagine that!

CHAPTER 11

Jesus—The Unforgettable Source and More Laws of His Spirit

The Bible says, "*And He* [Jesus] *is the head of the body, the church, who is the beginning, the firstborn from the dead, that in all things He may have the preeminence*" (Col. 1:18). In all things Jesus must have the preeminence. It's all about Him.

So when we're dealing with scriptural topics like the power of the imagination, we must remember that it's all about Him. We must focus on what He has said that He has in store for us so that we will become like Him.

You can't have all these wonderful things without Him. Without Him you can do nothing, but through Him you can do all things. He is the unforgettable Source of all the blessings we enjoy.

There is a great deal of research that corroborates the truth of the Word of God. This evidence shows that the Word is filled with truth. It is the living and breathing Word of God.

We must never divorce the Word from its source—Jesus of Nazareth who is a living Person. He is not some abstract universal principle. He is the Son of God, and His energy and power are available to believers today. In fact, He is the Word that became flesh and dwelt among us. (See John 1:14.)

THE HOPE OF GLORY

Some people get confused when they hear these words of Paul: "*...Christ in you, the hope of glory*" (Col. 1:27). Though Jesus lives within us and shares His glory with us, it is He who is divine, not us. He is leading us on a journey that is taking us from glory to glory and from faith to faith, however.

Throughout this process, though, we remain human beings, and there will always be a big difference between us and the Trinity. New Agers get confused about this distinction. Some will even say, "I am god" or "I am universal consciousness." These folk see God as the cosmic "It," not as a Person. The Word of God tells us that the Word (Jesus) became flesh and dwelt among us. He lived His life perfectly, as no one else has ever done. He gave His life on the Cross of Calvary and shed His blood to take away our sins. Then He rose from the dead so we would have abundant and eternal life with Him and thereby share in His glory throughout all eternity.

He glorifies our humanity and we partake of His nature, but we will never be God himself. The distinctive of our Christian life is that He shares His glory with us. This has been too often downplayed by a number of well-meaning people, including cultists, who have reduced His glory to certain principles. Certain higher-consciousness sects have done this, as well. And even some who call themselves Christians have done this.

As believers, however, we haven't used much of what the Bible tells us that we have in Christ. All too often the Word has been divorced from its Source. The Bible is not mythology nor is it a metaphor and a book of philosophical principles. It is a historical Word from God himself.

The events recorded in the Bible actually happened in our time-space world, but their meaning goes beyond the time-space world. This is vital to know when you enter into the realm of harvesting your dreams and developing the creative side of your mind. Whatever you pay attention to will take root and grow in your life.

For example, I think I need to transform the way my mind views my home state of New Jersey. Recently I read some slogans people had written about New Jersey. These were listed in a local newspaper. Let me share some of these humorous slogans with you:

New Jersey, what's it to you?
New Jersey, we'll tax the bleep out of you!
New Jersey, we're not as corrupt as we used to be.
All pay-offs gladly accepted here.
It's not as bad as it smells.

And for anyone who has driven the state's famous turnpike or the Garden State Parkway, *Welcome to New Jersey, expect delays.*

Can you imagine those slogans being posted on billboards in our state? These certainly are negative concepts of New Jersey, which we need to change before they actually become the absolute reality of life in our state. I want to see the glory of God come to New Jersey, so I have to change the way I think about my state. Of course, I have to deal with reality, but I realize at the same time that reality can be changed by changing the way we view things and letting our imaginations see things differently. We need to see and say what we want that reality to become.

SPIRITUAL DISCERNMENT

Paul writes, *"Now we have received, not the spirit of the world, but the Spirit who is from God, that we might know the things that have been freely given to us by God"* (1 Cor. 2:12). God has freely given us so much, and we gain access to those gifts through the Holy Spirit.

The apostle continues: *"These things we also speak, not in words which man's wisdom teaches but which the Holy Spirit teaches, comparing spiritual things with spiritual. But the natural man does not receive the things of the Spirit of God, for they are foolishness to him; nor can he know them, because they are spiritually discerned"* (1 Cor. 2:13-14).

There are spiritual laws that are in operation in the world and our personal lives. When we see and practice them, they work all the time just like physical laws do.

God is a Spirit and we connect with Him in the Spirit and in truth. We move in the Spirit, and we move also in truth. The Holy Spirit has a language, and His language often speaks in pictures to us. That is how He has made us. He wants us to experience His images, dreams, and visions. In this way He imparts truth to us.

You might say, "Well, I've been asking God for a lot of things, but I've received nothing."

I would answer, "But how do you ask?"

How do you ask the sun for sunlight? You just get out in the sun and experience it without asking. You walk out into the daylight. How do you ask electricity to give you light? You simply switch on the lamp, and you receive its light. In a similar vein, how do you ask God for what you want? You do so by getting in the Spirit and experiencing Him.

This is not natural. Too often people will run off and state their confessions before they have ever incubated the promises in their hearts or their imaginations. This is putting the cart before the horse.

Certain things, as Paul points out, are spiritually discerned. Your imagination is within your human spirit, and it has to be developed. There is a day when you can make confession with your mouth, but something must always precede your confession. You have to get into the Spirit. This is not something that God must do for you, but it does come from cooperating with Him. God is not some kind of a cosmic slot machine. He doesn't have favorites, and He doesn't operate by luck or chance. His spiritual laws work for anybody who knows how to use them properly.

Michael Jordan was not a professing Christian when he said, "I visualized myself as the kind of basketball player I wanted to be. I saw it every day in my imagination and I became that." By doing this he became the best basketball player who ever lived. There are great stars, and then there's Michael Jordan. Napoleon Hill, who wrote *Think and Grow*

Rich, used his imagination, and in his imagination he received helpful information from the sages of the ages. I don't know that Napoleon Hill was grounded in Jesus, but he discovered a power that is available to each of us.

There's a latent power in the human soul that everybody can use. God has freely given us things that will enable us to succeed, to be the head and not the tail. As we begin to realize this truth, we gird up the loins of our mind through repetition. You continue to imagine what you strongly desire until it takes root in your life. Those who are persistent with this are the ones who really see the desires of their life get fulfilled.

AN AGE OF DISCOVERY

Jesus said, *"Do not fear, little flock, for it is your Father's good pleasure to give you the kingdom"* (Luke 12:32). The age we're living in is an age of discovery. New planets, new life forms, new stars, new technologies, and new cures are being found. The only kind of discovery that is really new and different, however, is self-discovery.

Jesus said, *"You are the salt of the earth..."* (Matt. 5:13). The properties of salt include many things, such as cleansing, healing, purification, and seasoning. When you put a pinch of salt into a bowl of soup, its flavor changes. When you allow Jesus to use you as the salt of the earth, things and people around you will change. You will add flavor to life. Jesus wants to change everything about you. He wants you to be salty so that others will be thirsty for Him.

How does this happen? Jesus said that we need to follow His directions about praying, living, ministering, believing, and receiving. This will bring forth multiple changes in your life and the lives of others. The early disciples turned the world upside down. They spread the name of Jesus throughout the then-known world. They did mighty signs and wonders because they believed they were salt and light, and they knew Jesus had shared His glory with them. We can do the same.

THE SWORD OF TRUTH

The Bible says, "*You will chase your enemies, and they shall fall by the sword before you. Five of you shall chase a hundred, and a hundred of you shall put ten thousand to flight; your enemies shall fall by the sword before you*" (Lev. 26:7-8). This passage could well be referring to the sword of truth.

Take a look at what we could do by using the sword of truth together. God is saying that we shouldn't count according to actual numbers and we shouldn't look at the odds. He is saying, "If you use what I've given you, you're going to be mightier than any people on the earth." What a wonderful promise this is!

Could that be what Jesus was telling us through Paul, when he said that we are to enter the fullness of the stature of Jesus Christ? That's on this earth in the here-and-now, not just in Heaven. (See Ephesians 4:13.) This is God's goal for us, His family and His church.

How do you see truth? Often miracles are thought to be miracles because somebody does not understand the processes involved in bringing them to pass. In Jesus' day, if one of the disciples had pulled out a cell phone and started talking to somebody who was miles away, everybody would have thought that was a miracle. Today, however, it's the norm. If we go to the remote jungles of the Amazon, or to the aborigines of Australia, the airplane we use would be a miracle for those people, because they don't understand the laws of aerodynamics. Likewise, a television would be a miracle to them, because they don't know about broadcasting and sending signals through the air.

When you begin to understand and see how things work, what you may have thought was an impossibility or a miracle might well become a way of life. This is why I urge you to enter the spirit dimension, a place where you will receive from God. As you do so, that which used to look like a miracle might become an everyday experience for you.

The spiritual dimension is a place of faith. Will Jesus find faith in His people when He returns to earth? I believe He will, because I believe in His promise that the glory of the Lord will fill the earth as the waters cover the sea.

The Bride of Christ will be filled with faith and will be beautiful and radiant on the earth when Jesus returns. We're not completely there yet, but because we are able to see the ideal in our imaginations, we will not be depressed by the circumstances around us.

Keep God's ideals in front of you. Use your God-given imagination to see things as He sees them. This will bring forth life and creative power that will result in change. Remember that your subconscious mind is not reasonable. No idea can be expressed on the subconscious level before it is felt in the realm of your emotions. Then, when it is felt, it will take on dominion and authority. So what you feel is very real. What you feel may be good, bad, or indifferent, but what you feel on the inside will always find expression on the outside.

If this is so, how will you be able to control your feelings? This happens when you learn how to discipline your imagination. You must only entertain feelings that contribute to your joy and wholeness and other people's joy and wholeness. Do not dwell on imperfections and weaknesses within yourself or others. Eliminate the negative by accentuating the positive.

Your imagination always works on and from your dominant feelings. Let me give you an example. Saying, "I am healthy" is stronger in feeling than saying, "I will be healthy," for "I will be healthy" says, "I'm not healthy now." I don't feel as strong when I say that as I do when I declare that I am healthy. Positive declarations in the now of our lives make our expressed ideals become real in the realm of our imaginations. By doing so we're not denying what we see in my outer world right now. Instead, we're seeing ourselves (within our inner world) as though we are healthy and well now.

Let's say you are chained to a park bench and somebody comes along and says, "You've got to sit here for three hours and you can't move." In your mind and in your imagination you can say, "I'm going to run," and in your mind you will be running. You see, you're not chained to that park bench on the inside. Sensation always precedes manifestation, so be very watchful of your moods and your feelings. Always remember that there's an unbroken connection between your feelings and your visible world.

It has been reported that emotional disturbances that are unexpressed may lead to disease. That's why you can find overweight people who eat Twinkies twice a day even though they have high blood pressure, but they don't die of a stroke or a heart attack. Somehow they've found a way to express their feelings.

As believers, we have a wonderful and practical way to express our feelings, too—through praise and worship. Learn to express yourself and find effective ways to deal with the stuff on the inside. Make a mental shift and begin to think of positive outcomes, the way you and God really want to see things happen. See your desire being realized. Feel it and accept the mood it brings forth. When you do this, you're actually creating a mood for yourself.

It has been said that 99.9 percent of everything that happens to you doesn't happen by accident or because of some pre-determined fate. Most things happen as a result of your choices; in a sense, therefore, you create the things that happen. You begin by creating them in your mind and in your imagination.

For example, if you're feeling terribly guilty and you don't know how to deal with the guilt, you will begin looking for some kind of accident or something else to punish you. That can lead you in some very strange directions, and that's why you need the mind of Christ.

If you dwell on the difficulties of your life, or if you dwell on the barriers or delays you are experiencing with something, you will plant those related thoughts and feelings within your subconscious mind—your spirit-man. It will then receive and accept those thoughts and feelings. Eventually, it will proceed to produce them in your outer world.

Do you realize that your imagination is much like your spouse? You can't command him or her, can you? Or at least you'd better not try to do so! Instead, you may make gentle suggestions. You don't want to try to force your spouse with regard to anything. It is the same with your imagination. It can't be forced to comply with you. It has to come naturally in your spirit. As you persevere, that sacred moment will come. That one beautiful moment that the devil knows nothing about will surely come.

Though the devil can hear your words, he can't get into your mind and your imagination. Once you give birth to something in your imagination, and cultivate it each day through prayer, it will be done. It will happen. In the secret place of prayer, the eyes of your heart will open and you will begin to see things through the power of your imagination.

The time you spend alone with God in the secret place is like a honeymoon in which the bride gets to know the bridegroom. Love blossoms into full bloom, and great expectancy arises in your heart. Then the picture you are focusing on in your imagination will become a seed that will actually impregnate your imagination with what God wants to bring forth.

You'll never be the same after that, for you will leave the chamber pregnant. And after the time of gestation, you'll give birth to a visible demonstration of your heart's desire, but understand that this won't happen immediately. The birthing of your desires will be a time of great rejoicing.

Yes, you will leave there changed, for you will be impregnated with the seed of God. The strong, God-given desires that you allow yourself to feel and realize will seem to have already been fulfilled. Then you won't have to long for them anymore, for they are within you. Then you will nurture those desires by girding up the loins of your mind. You will keep declaring it to yourself in your mind; then you will actually speak the word forth.

Prayer is like God's marriage ceremony. When we begin to enjoy it, things always happen. And why not enjoy it? You can have fun with God. At His right hand there is fullness of joy and pleasures forevermore. Enjoy the honeymoon; then wait for the exciting moment of birth. In your dream life, in your imagination you can have it now. Before you go to bed at night, say to the Lord, "Jesus, I see this desire fulfilled and I'm going to receive this thing right now," and it will start to penetrate your dream life. Remember, Jesus is your Source for everything that's good.

Get alone with God in the secret place, and satan will know nothing about it. Be sure not to open your mouth prematurely, however. Share these deeper things of God only with close friends or family members who are on the same page as you. Don't try to impress your friends by telling them what God is going to do. Let it incubate within the womb of your spirit.

Remember how the Holy Spirit brooded over the chaos until God's creative word was spoken? God spoke and all creation came forth. You must wait before the Lord in prayer, brooding over that which He is about to create.

There's some selfishness in prayer, if only in the joy and pleasure you receive when you see answers to your prayers. Ask God, "What do You want in my life?" He will show you and He will begin to open the eyes of your heart (your imagination). Then you will be able to pray fervently, expectantly, and earnestly. You'll be able to say, "I can dream! All things are possible."

In the process don't totally put aside the logical side of your mind. Don't become some kind of oddball glowing in the dark. We don't need more of those. We need people who will worship God with their minds and use their intellects for His glory. But don't forget to develop your imagination at the same time. Begin to see your friends and family members coming to the Lord. Begin to see your dream being fulfilled and your desires being realized.

And if you've had a bad conversation with someone who doesn't know the Lord, erase that memory tape and replay it with new words. Hear them say, "I'm interested in what you have to say." Your imagination will pick that up and it will begin to manifest what you are saying and thinking. Then, sometime later, you will find greater openness toward the Gospel of Jesus Christ in that person's heart.

That's the power you have in the Holy Spirit. The day will come when you will be able to confess your expectations, because the desire is in you and you feel it strongly. You will give birth to it and it will become manifest to the outside world. Now imagine that!

I'm sure you are excited about some of the new things you have learned in this book. As my favorite preacher, T.D. Jakes, says, "Get ready, get ready, get ready!" You are manifesting new and wonderful things already, because the revelation knowledge of Jesus has brought you much closer to your fulfilled destiny. Now you are imagining that which He promised—abundant life in this world and the one to come. I will see you at the top of your dream. Now, continue to imagine that!